# Coding for Communicators

An Easy-to-Follow, Fast-Learn
Course in XML, HTML, and CSS

**Carly Finseth, Ph.D.**

thoughtsuite

# TABLE OF CONTENTS

# CHAPTER 1
# GETTING STARTED

## Introduction

I built my first website in the Fall of 2000 after finding a few interesting books on HTML during a trip to Barnes and Noble. I was eager to try this new trend. However, when I got home and tried the books in practice, it was confusing and filled with technical jargon. I had to start somewhere, though, so I muddled my way through designing and publishing my first site.

I enjoyed learning HTML so much that I started creating content simply to fill web pages. I felt a rush every time I worked with new text and image layouts on the screen. Something about seeing words and pictures I created show up on a computer screen opened a new world of communication. I was expressing myself visually, through code, for the world to see.

I experimented with creating interactive content that allowed for others to comment on my site and contribute their own work. As the site grew, I became less interested in creating the content myself and more interested in helping others communicate their ideas. The result was an online magazine, *Empowerment4Women*, that I ran for more than 11 years, overseeing more than 30 issues, 10 regular columnists, and dozens of individual contributors.

It was a painstaking process for me to learn HTML but it was so worth it. The digital literacy I built for myself more than two decades ago still helps today as I muddle through customizing a WordPress theme or playing with a new website design in HTML5.

It was also a slippery slope. I fell in love with coding websites so completely that it became a hobby to create them for fun. I've since built dozens of websites for myself and friends, from personal portfolios to blogs, ecommerce sites to business promotional sites. I also grew my skill set to learn not just HTML but also CSS and JavaScript, as well as the most popular CMS (content management systems) such as WordPress and Joomla!. As I learned, I also took my skills offline and built knowledge in XML, as well as Python. But the thing is: I'm not a professional coder. I just know enough to be dangerous.

Understanding basic coding techniques has helped me countless times in terms of both time and money. It's also benefited me in the various jobs I've held—from teaching in higher education to working in corporate executive positions. Knowing just enough to talk the talk has helped me bridge communication gaps across academic and corporate departments, which has led to improvements in interpersonal relationships, political capital, and productivity.

This book is the culmination of my decades of personal experience, as well as months of research dedicated to helping students in technical communication and other humanities fields learn more about coding.

Knowing just enough to get by—and therefore learning and understanding key terms and concepts of a technical field—is a skill that is valued in most professional settings, as it increases communication and empathy. If you can understand the needs of the customers while also talking the talk with the engineers and coders creating the tools and software, you can place yourself in a very powerful position for promoting positive change.

This is the heart of technical communication: understanding technical concepts enough to communicate them to the end users in a way that is empathetic, clear, and concise. It's a humanistic approach to technology that makes technical communicators experts in user advocacy.

I first wrote much of the content in this book for graduate students in technical communication, with a focus on teaching them tools and technologies they would need to be successful on the job market. I wanted to teach a graduate-level course on coding for absolute beginners but I couldn't find a textbook I liked to do the job.

Most of the books I found on coding were aimed at people who already think like a coder. Many texts were too technical right from the start and if they "dumbed things down" it came across as condescending to adult learners. Therefore, I did what any sane professor would do with their summer downtime: I wrote the book myself.

First, though, I had to be sure my idea was relevant. I spent weeks researching blogs, articles, and job ads to discover the latest trends in workplace communication. I wanted to know: What tools and technologies would best serve students to have on their resumes when looking to find a job?

One topic that came up again and again was coding. I knew from talking with my students they had the desire to learn to code but not much time. Most of them were working full-time while taking graduate courses on the side, and there simply wasn't time in my class to become expert coders overnight. However, I was confident that with the right tools — such as textbooks, projects, and hands-on opportunities for learning — my students could walk away with at least a foundational understanding of coding for technical communicators.

Once I had settled on the topics for the course, I thought building the projects and assignments would be easy. However, I had a terrible time finding the appropriate-level coding books for absolute beginners. I was dismayed at how many books on XML or HTML didn't even begin with the basics, such as: What is XML and what can you do with it?

They instead would jump right in with tools and coder speak, which I knew would be completely overwhelming to my students. Some books were even worse: they came with the assumption that the user already was familiar with HTML or another coding language such as C or Java. I knew I could build lectures around the topics but I didn't feel that would be the best way to learn coding. I wanted my students to have something in their hands that they could read and experiment with at their own pace. But since the readings didn't exist as far as I could tell, I had to create them myself.

This book is the result of this adventure in teaching absolute beginners — and specifically, beginners who are communicators not coders — how to code. I wrote this book to teach students about coding in a way that answers the basic questions, such as "What is XML?" and "What Does XML Do?" and also provides real-world examples of XML in action. I wrote it to provide foundational understanding of common tools needed for professional technical communicators, but it is also useful for people in professions such as marketing, public relations, usability and user experience, project management, and more.

If you're a humanist who would like to learn about coding, this book is for you.

## What to Expect in This Book

Before we begin, let me emphasize the content in this book has been designed for an absolute beginner. You do not have to have any experience at all in coding languages or programming to succeed and learn.

This book is intended to be as hands-on as possible, so be prepared to follow along on your own device or computer as you learn. I'll provide you with links to free and available tools and technologies so you can learn right alongside the examples provided.

Every project you take on in this book will go a bit like this:

What are the very basics I need to know for this topic?

What can I create to demonstrate this new skill/knowledge?

Which advanced activities can I complete to demonstrate expertise in the topic? And which could I potentially showcase on a resume or in a professional portfolio?

You're welcome to jump around from project to project, depending on your interests and depending on how well you feel you're learning the subject. Do not get frustrated if at first this is a bit difficult; just like all worthwhile endeavors it's supposed to be somewhat hard. However, also recognize that you're accomplishing something great. If you can understand enough coding to get by, you'll already be ahead of many others in your field.

You won't find vocabulary here that is unexplained or over your head. As adult learners, you also won't be condescended to or called a "dummy." What you will find are practical applications with real-world examples you can try at home. If you're a lifelong learner with an enthusiasm for tackling new technologies and ideas, you'll find this book to be a guide alongside your own journey of learning new things.

## Why Learn to Code if You're Not a Coder?

If you're working in or adjacent to a technical industry, you're exposed to coding. Programmers, engineers, and software developers are consistently creating and updating apps and technologies to improve our lives. However, what they do doesn't happen in a vacuum; they need communications and usability professionals to help sell, teach, and market their products to the masses. While communications professionals don't need to be whiz coders, in my opinion they do have an obligation to understand enough about the topic to be good at their jobs. They need to understand just enough to communicate with both the engineers and developers who create the code, as well as the consumers, users, and general public who use the end products. In other words, they need to know just enough to be effective translators and user advocates.

Tom Johnson, a technical writer and blogger on "I'd Rather Be Writing," has noted coding as one of the top technical communication trends for the past couple of years—and the trend isn't expected to slow down any time soon. Even Forbes has recognized the trend; in their article entitled "8 Jobs That Are Easier to Land If You Can Code," the first job was technical writing. (Almost all of the other careers listed are also technical communication jobs, including: instructional designer, user experience designer, and product manager.) This isn't to say, though, that you must be a programmer to be a good technical writer, or even that you have to write any code at all. What it does mean is you should understand how to read code in certain languages. You should be able to traverse enough of it to write high quality documentation, tutorials, manuals, guides, and other technical communication artifacts, as well as effectively communicate with the software engineers and programmers who are experts in coding.

In other words: You've gotta know just enough to get by.

In this book, you'll learn the basics of the following programming languages: (1) XML; (2) HTML; and (3) CSS. These languages weren't chosen by accident, as they are learnable, usable, and—most especially—relevant to current trends and careers in technical communication, marketing, user experience, and more. The goal by the end of this book is for you to have at least a working knowledge—that is, to be able to read and write at a basic level—in these programming languages.

## What are XML and HTML?

XML (eXtensible Markup Language) and its cousin HTML (Hypertext Markup Language) have long been cornerstones for technical communication. Each, as their names suggest, are markup languages—meaning they are designed to help you "markup" (or style, format, and organize) written content. XML is most commonly used for single-sourcing technical communication content in both digital and print format (meaning: you write it once, and then format and output it several different ways); whereas HTML is used to build websites. Both are widely applicable to what you do—or will do—in a career in technical communication. Although you don't need to be an expert by any means, many technical writers find themselves writing and/or reading in at least basic to intermediate levels of either or both of these coding languages in their day-to-day jobs.

## Stuff to Do Before You Begin

First, get your tools. This book focuses on various tools and technologies; as such, you'll need a computer that's capable of running a variety of programs and interfaces. A PC or Mac is best; however, a Chromebook will work in most instances, although you may have to modify a few exercises to fit your technology. I'll walk you through all of that in the chapters that follow. For now, make sure you have access to a desktop or laptop computer (or a Chromebook, if that's all you have), as well as web browsers, a text editor, and an XML editor.

Details are below.

## Installing Web Browsers

Internet browsers are funny little things; not all code works in every browser. Therefore, I recommend that you install at least two different browsers on every machine that you will use for coding in this book. If you have issues with one, try another—and always try to view your completed code in more than one browser, so you can see if and how it will shift from user to user.

Here are a few browsers to try:

**Firefox** (www.mozilla.org) is often hailed as one of the friendliest browsers for coders; it tends to be quite forgiving, even if you have some errors.

**Internet Explorer** (www.microsoft.com) is outdated and can be a bit clunky for surfing the web IMHO, but tends (at least for me) to be one of the most reliable browsers for testing a variety of code.

**Edge** (www.microsoft.com) is Microsoft's newest answer to web browsing but, again IMHO, has some bugs that makes testing code somewhat unreliable. You're welcome to try it, though, if you're a fan of the interface and browser.

**Safari** (www.apple.com) is the go-to browser for Mac products—but full disclosure: I don't have experience testing code with this browser, as I'm a PC user.

**Chrome** (www.google.com) is the least forgiving of the Internet browsers, but may work for you depending on which version of code you're working on and what version of the browser you're using.

*Note: A known common error when coding in Chrome is for the code to come up as blank. If this happens, you may need to make sure you're using the latest version of Chrome. If that still doesn't work, try a second browser.*

If you want to get really fancy, you can also try a variety of web developer add-ons for various browsers, which allows for more advanced features. They aren't necessary for this book—but if you're interested and enjoy playing with new tools and technologies, you may want to read this article and check some out: https://forum.freecodecamp.org/t/which-browser-has-the-best-developer-tools-and-explain-why/2025.

## Choosing a Text Editor

Text editors are just that: tools to edit text. You will need a good text editor if you want to tackle the coding projects in this book. Text editors are used for coding, markup, and writing. In other words, they're perfect tools to have at the top of your technical communication toolkit!

# CODING FOR COMMUNICATORS

Here are some recommended text editors:

**Notepad++**: A free source code and text editor. This is my favorite tool and is recommended if you have a Windows computer. It is like Notepad (which is likely already installed on your machine) but has built in capabilities that are handy for coding, including color labeling and the capacity for multiple windows to be open at once. Download at www.notepad-plus-plus.org.

**Sublime Text**: Another free text and source code editor. I personally don't care for the aesthetics (black background, white and colored text), but many coders love and prefer this tool. It's purely a personal choice. It's available for both Windows and OS X (10.7 or later). Download at www.sublimetext.com.

**Brackets**: A free text editor from Adobe. If you're an Adobe person (e.g., Creative Suite) the interface and design of this editor may seem familiar to you. Download at www.brackets.io.

**Atom**: Yet another free text editor. I haven't yet tried this one personally, but a former student recommended it to me as a good option. Download at www.atom.io.

**Caret**: Although I haven't used this, it's a top choice if you're coding on a Chromebook. Download from the Chrome Web Store at www.chrome.google.com.

***Tip***: *See this website for some additional resources if you have a Chromebook:* *https://www.makeuseof.com/tag/four-best-text-editors-chromebook/*.

## Learning Advanced XML Editors

Most companies that write XML as part of their technical documentation strategy use an XML editor. The problem (for us) is that these software packages are often ridiculously expensive—usually several hundred to several thousand dollars per license.

However, I still want you to learn how such programs work. Learning at least one of them will get you familiar with what these tools do and will provide you with the skill set needed to then apply this knowledge to any other similar software.

See below for your options while working through the materials in this book. Note that both come with free trials you can use while working through the learning activities.

Here are some recommended XML editing software packages:

**MadCap Flare**: This is a professional software package used by many professional technical writers. Start here, if you can. However, they only have a free 30-day trial. After that, the cost is (hang on, while I puke a little): nearly $1,500. They do have educational pricing if you have an .edu email address, but you will need to contact them to find out what that is. Find more information at www.madcapsoftware.com.

**Adobe FrameMaker**: An alternative to MadCap Flare, Adobe FrameMaker does have a free trial as well. At the time of this writing, paid licenses are $999.00 for the full software or $29.99 a month to subscribe, with educational pricing for $399.00 (or $699.00 if you want to add RoboHelp). Find more information at www.adobe.com/products/framemaker.html.

## Some Optional Reading

Everything you need to get started coding XML, HTML, and CSS is in this book—and we'll get started in the next chapter so feel free to go there now.

However, I *am* a professor at heart, so if you're interested in reading more (yay! reading!) on the importance of coding for non-coders, here are some additional sources you may want to check out.

*Coding Literacy: How Computer Programming is Changing Writing* **by Annette Vee**

> **Why to read it**: This is an excellent book that highlights the crossover between the humanities and the sciences, and why communications professionals and other humanists should pay attention to coding. Buy it online at Amazon.com and at other retailers.

## CODING FOR COMMUNICATORS

**"How Can a Technical Writer Develop a Love of Programming Code?" by Tom Johnson**

> **Why to read it:** This is an article that scratches the surface of the importance of coding for technical communicators and others in adjacent careers. Find it at: https://idratherbewriting.com/2013/04/18/how-can-a-technical-writer-develop-a-love-a-programming-code/.

After you have your tools gathered and have done all the reading you're in the mood for, meet me in the next chapter to get started.

# CHAPTER 2
# INTRODUCTION TO XML

## What You'll Learn

- What is XML?
- What does XML do—and what can you do with it?
- Why is XML valuable for technical communicators, marketers, usability professionals, and other non-coders?

## What You'll Create

By the end of this chapter, you will have created a few lines of XML code from scratch to prepare you to move forward to Chapter 3.

## Required Tools and Supplies

You will need access to a good text editor, such as Notepad++, as well as access to at least one web browser. See Chapter 1 for download information.

## What is XML?

XML (eXtensible Markup Language) is a coding language that is used to communicate and organize data. It is one of several markup languages used to communicate and categorize data in digital formats, primarily on the Internet.

Okay, back up. What is a markup language?

A markup language is a coding language used primarily for the web. It consists of rules and tags, and is a way of categorizing, processing, and presenting information. Examples of markup languages include XML, XHTML, and HTML.

Gotcha. Now, **what is a tag?**

A tag is something that is enclosed between two brackets, like this: < >. Examples of tags include: <topic>, <content>, and <category>. In markup languages like HTML, the tags are predefined, meaning the language has a set of codes that you *must* use in order for the HTML to work. (Don't worry; you'll learn about that starting in Chapter 5.) The best part about XML is you create the tags yourself, based on whatever naming conventions make the most sense to you.

This, by the way, is why XML is called an "eXtensible" markup language: it can be *extended* to suit your own customized needs.

In XML there are two types of tags:

- The **start tag**, which looks like this: <tag>

- The **end tag**, which includes a forward slash, like this: </tag>

Tags are used to categorize your content. You might think of them as labels. The primary content of what you're writing goes between the opening tag and the closing tag.

## Example

Below is an example of what an XML document may look like to organize the employee names, job titles, and salaries for a Research and Development division of a fictional software company named Content Penguin.

```
<company name="Content Penguin">
    <department name="Research and
Development">
        <employee>
            <name>Kayla
Stevens</name>
            <job>Software
Analyst</job>
            <salary>60000</salary>
        </employee>
    </department>
</company>
```

Here, we have defined six different tags: <company>, <department>, <employee>, <name>, <job>, and <salary>. The <company> start tag is at the beginning of the XML, as all of the other information is a part of the company's information. This is why the other tags are enclosed (or "nested") within it. The <department> tag is nested within the <company> tag, the <employee> tag is nested within the <department> tag, and so on.

Note that every **start tag** must also have an **end tag**, to tell the computer where the associated information starts and stops. Whatever content you place between the start tag and the end tag will be defined by the document as the content for that tag.

This also demonstrates the importance of **data hierarchy** and **structure** within an XML document. XML, like any coding language, is logical and ordered. The order in which you place information, and its relation to itself and other information in the document matters; empty spaces (or lack thereof) also matter. (Note, for instance, how there are no spaces before or after the = sign in the code.)

When you work on your own XML, be sure to follow the "rules" of the code exactly, and don't erroneously add or take out spaces where necessary, or you may discover you have errors.

To that end, coding XML—like any code—is also about attention to detail. You'll see in ongoing levels and other projects in this book that a fun part of coding is **debugging,** or discovering and correcting errors. This is much like copyediting. As you progress in this course, you'll learn when to recognize when something is wrong in a particular set of code and how to fix it.

-ᗆ- *Tip: In the previous example, you might also notice that each major category has been tabbed over; that is, the major categories are indented. This isn't required for XML code to work, but it helps you as the coder recognize where each major section of code starts and stops. I highly recommend you use indenting in your own code —whether XML, HTML, Python, or other language—as a way to help yourself organize your information.*

## What Does XML Do?

Well, first let's start with what XML does *not* do. XML does not format text. It does not apply styles such as color, font, bold or italics, or layout. XML isn't concerned about what the data looks like. It's simply concerned about presenting data that can be easily read and interpreted by both humans and computers.

What XML *does* do is organize information. It helps machines and web browsers read information and then translates it back in a way that makes logical, organized sense.

In short, it places a distinction between **content** and **format**.

## Why Do Technical Communicators Use XML?

XML is a powerful way to **communicate**, **distribute**, and **single-source** information. (Single-sourcing lets you reproduce the same exact content across various modes of output, such as print and digital.) Because XML doesn't worry about how pretty something may look (as opposed to, say, HTML), it is only concerned with *data*.

XML is also **text-based**; it does not include images, styles, or formatting. Therefore, it is a good choice for when you are working with a lot of data that could be messed up if used with a particular operating system or browser. Because it is only text, every machine, system, and browser can read it without errors.

XML also helps writers **standardize information**. Therefore, it's a popular choice for composing information that could frequently change, such as product or software documentation.

Take, for example, a manual that is available both in print PDF and on a webpage. If the technical writer composes it traditionally, they will have one manual they've created in word processing software (to create the PDF) and one they've created in a web editor (to create the HTML or other web-based code). When the manual needs to be changed, they'll have to update the information in both platforms and formats.

Instead, the technical writer could use XML to compose the information in just one document. Whenever the content needs to be updated, they would just update it *once*—in XML. It would be up to the various output machines to render it for the various formats. You'll learn more on how that is done in the next section.

## How Do You Transform and Format XML?

Because XML is simply text-based, you need something else to tell the computer what to do with the data. This is through the use of stylesheets, otherwise known as XSL (eXtensible Stylesheet Language). XSL gives the XML a *style*; it makes the XML look pretty.

XSL does two things to the data in the XML file:

- *Transforms* the data; and

- *Formats* the data.

**Transforming** the data means that it translates the data from XML to your preferred output format (e.g. PDF or HTML).

**Formatting** the data means giving it style and design (e.g., giving it a font style, a background color, or bolding).

However, before your computer can transform and format your data, you must give it some commands so it knows what to do. You first do this by telling it to reference a separate XSL stylesheet. In short:

- The **XML document** (.xml) is where you write, organize, and name your data.

- The **XSL stylesheet** (.xsl or .xslt) is a separate document in which you write commands for transforming and formatting the data in your XML document.

Then, you need to go back to your XML document and tell the computer where to find the associated XSL stylesheet. That's what we'll learn to do below.

## Example of an XML Document with an Associated XSL Stylesheet

Here's the same example we looked at previously, but with a few new lines of code at the top. These two new lines finalize the XML and tell the computer where to find the associated XSL stylesheet.

```
<?xml version="1.0" encoding="ISO-8859-
1"?>
<?xml-stylesheet type="text/xsl"
href="example01.xslt"?>
<company name="Content Penguin">
    <department name="Research and
Development">
        <employee>
            <name>Kayla
Stevens</name>
            <job>Software
Analyst</job>
            <salary>60000</salary>
        </employee>
    </department>
</company>
```

What we've done is add two lines to the top of the document, to tell your computer what type of code to expect and how to read it.

The first line of code is called the **XML declaration**. It is the first line of an XML document and is required for the machine to understand and read your code as XML. It tells your computer which version of XML you're using; in this case, you're using version 1.0.

Optionally, you may also tell the computer what type of encoding (or character language) to use. Here, we're using ISO-8859-1, which is a single-byte encoding that can represent the first 256 unicode characters.

*-ᗰ- **Tip**: For the purposes of this book, I suggest you save the following line of code and copy it into the top of every single XML document you create:*

```
<?xml version="1.0" encoding="ISO-8859-1"?>
```

The second line of code is the **stylesheet declaration**. It tells the computer where and how to find your stylesheet, or the document we'll create next to instruct the computer how to transform and format your data.

```
<?xml-stylesheet type="text/xsl" href="example01.xslt"?>
```

This line of code is saying:

Dear XML document,

I would like to use an XSL stylesheet to format my data.

The stylesheet will be in text format, written in XSL (.xsl or .xslt).

The name of my XSL stylesheet is called "example01.xslt." You can find it in the same folder as this XML document I'm typing in.

Love, Coder

Of course, the callout "example01.xslt" will change, depending on the name of your XSL stylesheet. And, it's possible that the location would change, if you saved it somewhere else on your computer.

For now, to keep things simple, save your XML stylesheets in the same folder that you have created your XML documents.

 *Tip: Always use lowercase letters when naming files—regardless of what you're coding. Also avoid the use of spaces or special characters.*

## Creating the XSL Stylesheet

Now that you've told your XML document to find and read from an XSL stylesheet, you need to create that stylesheet.

Here's an example of what the associated XSL stylesheet may look like, in order to transform and format the XML data:

```
<?xml version="1.0" encoding="ISO-8859-
1"?>
<xsl:stylesheet version="1.0"
xmlns:xsl="http://www.w3.org/1999/XSL/T
ransform">
<xsl:template match="/">
<table border="1">
    <tr>
        <th>Employee Name</th>
```

```
        <th>Job Title</th>
        <th>Annual Salary</th>
    </tr>
    <tr>
        <td><xsl:value-of
select="/company/department/employee/na
me"/></td>
        <td><xsl:value-of
select="/company/department/employee/jo
b"/></td>
        <td><xsl:value-of
select="/company/department/employee/sa
lary"/></td>
    </tr>
</table>
</xsl:template>
</xsl:stylesheet>
```

Now let's take a detailed look at the code in the above stylesheet.

## Declaration and Namespace

Just like in your XML document, the first line is the declaration. It is required for the machine to understand and read your code. Just like before, this example is telling your computer that you're using XML version 1.0, and, again, we're using ISO-8859-1 encoding:

```
<?xml version="1.0" encoding="ISO-8859-
1"?>
```

The second line of code is called the **XML namespace**. The XML namespace (or **xmlns**) helps your computer and any human readers know which naming conventions you've used in the document. In this example, it means the code and naming conventions used on that page have been written using the guidelines found at the website http://www.w3.org/1999/XSL/Transform.

```
<xsl:stylesheet version="1.0"
xmlns:xsl="http://www.w3.org/1999/XSL/T
ransform">
```

*Note: This is almost always the website and conventions used in XSL stylesheets. Feel free to click through and see the universal standards for creating XSL documents; however, it's not necessary that you know nor even really understand any of the information there for the purposes of this book—and even to use XML and XSL in practice.*

The third line of code defines what is called the **XML template**. This is a way for you to define templates for formatting your information—including which portions of your XML to select and format. For now, we're using the code "/" which is a generic code for telling the XSL stylesheet to select and format everything in the XML document:

```
<xsl:template match="/">
```

As you get more advanced using XML and XSL, you can define multiple layers of templates and styles to documents. However, you can still do some fairly complex formatting and transforming without needing to do so.

For the purposes of this book (and even beyond), I suggest you save the following three lines of code (the declaration, the namespace, and the template) and copy/paste them at the start of every XSL stylesheet you create:

```
<?xml version="1.0" encoding="ISO-8859-
1"?>
<xsl:stylesheet version="1.0"
xmlns:xsl="http://www.w3.org/1999/XSL/T
ransform">
<xsl:template match="/">
```

## XML Data Output

Next, we get to the heart of what we want the XSL stylesheet to output and format for us. In our example, we want our data to be transformed and formatted into HTML, so we can read it in a web browser or use it on a website. Therefore, to make this happen, we use HTML in the next portion of the code:

```
<table border="1">
  <tr>
    <th>Employee Name</th>
    <th>Job Title</th>
    <th>Annual Salary</th>
  </tr>
  <tr>
```

```
    <td><xsl:value-of
select="/company/department/employee/name"
/></td>
    <td><xsl:value-of
select="/company/department/employee/job"/
></td>
 <td><xsl:value-of
select="/company/department/employee/salar
y"/></td>
    </tr>
</table>
```

The start tag **<table>** tells the computer to create a table for the information. The code **border="1"** tells the computer to put a border that is 1 pixel (px) wide around the table.

The next line is **<tr>**, which is the tag for a new row for a table.

The tag of **<th>** is the  tag for creating a new header for the table. In this case, the headers for the table will be called "Employee Name," "Job Title," and "Annual Salary."

**</tr>** is the ending code for the <tr> table row, so it's telling the computer to end the row.

The new **<tr>** tells the computer to create the next row.

**<td>** is the code for creating a new cell in a table row. Note that we also must remember to use an end tag </td> to end the content of each cell.

(Neato! You just learned some HTML code! <table>, <tr>, and <td> are all HTML tags that we're using to format our XML data into an HTML web page.)

This next part is where the XML data gets pulled in from your XML document.

Take this code, for example:

```
<xsl:value-of
select="/company/department/employee/na
me"/>
```

This tells the computer to go find the information from your XML sheet that you've put between the **<name>** start tag and the **</name>** end tag, and put that data in the first table's cell. (In our example, the computer would find and return the name Kayla Stevens.)

Likewise, the next two lines would retrieve the information between your <job> and </job> tags and put in the table's second cell, and then retrieve the information between your <salary> and </salary> tags and put it in the table's third cell.

```
<xsl:value-of
select="/company/department/employee/jo
b"/>
<xsl:value-of
select="/company/department/employee/sa
lary"/>
```

## Finishing Touches

Note that at the end of each table cell, we must remember to also close the tag with </td>, which tells the computer that it's done reading the information for that particular table cell.

Likewise, when we're done with the table row, we need to remember to close it with the </tr> tag. Then, we need to end the entire table by using the </table> end tag.

As a final step we must also remember to close the tags for the XSL template and stylesheet, as follows:

```
</xsl:template>
</xsl:stylesheet>
```

Ta-da! Your first XSL stylesheet is complete. Next you'll learn to replicate the above actions, make the code your own, and then test it in a web browser.

## Writing Your First Lines of XML

Now that you have a basic understanding of what XML is and how it's used, it's time to showcase what you've learned. To do so, follow the below instructions.

## Step 1: Create Your XML Document

- Open up Notepad++ or your text editor of choice.

- Create a new document.

- Copy the below code and then save it as company.xml.

```xml
<?xml version="1.0" encoding="ISO-8859-1"?>
<?xml-stylesheet type="text/xsl"
href="example01.xslt"?>
<company name="Content Penguin">
  <department name="Research and
Development">
    <employee>
      <name>Kayla Stevens</name>
      <job>Software Analyst</job>
      <salary>60000</salary>
    </employee>
  </department>
</company>
```

## Step 2: Create Your XSL Stylesheet

- Once again open Notepad++ or your text editor of choice.

- Create another new document.

- Copy the below code and then save it as example01.xslt.

```
<?xml version="1.0" encoding="ISO-8859-1"?>
<xsl:stylesheet version="1.0"
xmlns:xsl="http://www.w3.org/1999/XSL/Transf
orm">
<xsl:template match="/">
<table border="1">
  <tr>
    <th>Employee Name</th>
    <th>Job Title</th>
    <th>Annual Salary</th>
  </tr>
  <tr>
    <td><xsl:value-of
select="/company/department/employee/name"/>
</td>
    <td><xsl:value-of
select="/company/department/employee/job"/><
/td>
    <td><xsl:value-of
select="/company/department/employee/salary"
/></td>
  </tr>
</table>
</xsl:template>
</xsl:stylesheet>
```

# Step 3: Test the Code

- Open up your web browser of choice.

*Note*: *Google Chrome is notorious for having issues with reading XML and XSL stylesheets on a local computer, due to their security features. I recommend using Internet Explorer or Firefox first.*

- Use the command Ctrl-O on your computer to open a file in your web browser. (If your browser doesn't have that feature, try File --> Open, or search online for how to open files in your specific web browser.

- Navigate to where you saved your company.xml file from Step 1 and double-click to open it. You should see something that looks like this:

| Employee Name | Job Title | Annual Salary |
|---|---|---|
| Kayla Stevens | Software Analyst | 60000 |

*Important Note*: *Testing your code is something you will do perhaps more than anything else while working on learning new coding languages. Be sure to spend time getting comfortable with opening files in web browsers, making small tweaks, and then reloading your code.*

*-* *Tip:* *Every time you try something new with your code, you will have to reload it in your web browser to get it to notice your changes. In most browsers, you can do this by selecting F5. If that doesn't work, try Ctrl-F5. And if that still doesn't work, you may have to close your browser and re-open it. (Ah, yes. The joys of technology.) I highly recommend that as you're learning new coding skills — and even when you become more advanced — that you reopen and/or refresh your code every single time you make even the smallest of changes. That way, if something breaks or doesn't work correctly, you'll be able to more easily tell which portion of the code is causing the issues.*

## Step 4: Create Your Own Fictional Scenario and Rewrite the XML

- Go back to your text editor and create a copy of the code from company.xml.

- Think of a new fictional scenario and rewrite the data so it suits this new narrative.

- Save your new XML file as something new, still remembering to end it with the .xml extension. Save it in the same place where you've kept your company.xml file and your example01.xslt stylesheet.

**Example**

For instance, in company.xml I used the fictional software company Content Penguin, and looked at the name, job, and salary of an employee in their Research and Development division. To rewrite it, I've decided to create a fictional movie studio and look at one of their top-grossing films. My rewritten code now looks like this:

```
<?xml version="1.0" encoding="ISO-8859-1"?>
<?xml-stylesheet type="text/xsl"
href="example02.xslt"?>
  <studio name="Brilliant Studios">
    <department name="Production">
      <movie>
      <name>Love Story Number Nine</name>
      <star>Julie Robertson</star>
      <boxoffice>$265,000,099</boxoffice>
      </movie>
    </department>
  </studio>
```

You'll notice I changed every part of the fictional example except for the tag <department>, since that still fit my fictional scenario. Also note that although "box office" is normally two words, here I've made it one word, as **XML tags should be lowercase with no spaces or special characters**. (If you want to delineate between multiple words, it is allowable to use underscores; for instance, I could have made this: <box_office>.)

Also note this time I used a dollar sign ($) and commas for the box office numbers. These symbols are allowed because they're part of the data itself, not the tag.

I then saved the above in a new .xml file I titled movies.xml.

Finally, I changed the name of the stylesheet to example02.xslt. We will create that new stylesheet in the next step.

# Step 5: Revise Your XSL Stylesheet

- Go back to your text editor and create a copy of the code from example01.xslt. Save it as a new file named example02.xslt. Be sure to save it in the same folder where you saved your new .xml file in Step 4.

- Rewrite the code in the XSL stylesheet so the naming conventions match what you did in your XML revisions from Step 4.

- Click "Save" to keep your changes.

**Example**

Using my new example from Step 4, I would now change the XSL stylesheet code to match the new language I've used to tag my data (e.g., studio, department, movie, name, star, and boxoffice).

Here is what my revised code now looks like:

```
<?xml version="1.0" encoding="ISO-8859-1"?>
<xsl:stylesheet version="1.0"
xmlns:xsl="http://www.w3.org/1999/XSL/Transf
orm">
<xsl:template match="/">
```

```
<table border="1">
  <tr>
    <th>Movie Name</th>
    <th>Starring Role</th>
    <th>Box Office Sales</th>
  </tr>
  <tr>
    <td><xsl:value-of
select="/studio/department/movie/name"/></td
>
    <td><xsl:value-of
select="/studio/department/movie/star"/></td
>
    <td><xsl:value-of
select="/studio/department/movie/boxoffice"/
></td>
  </tr>
</table>
</xsl:template>
</xsl:stylesheet>
```

Note how I changed the headings of each row to "Movie Name," "Starring Role," and "Box Office Sales." I also changed the xsl:value-of section by renaming the hierarchical conventions I created in my new fictional scenario. Instead of company/department/employee, for instance, I now need it to follow studio/department/movie.

## Step 6: Test Your Revised Documents

- Once again, open up your web browser of choice.

- Use the command Ctrl-O on your computer to open up the new .xml file in your web browser. (If your browser doesn't have that feature, try File --> Open, or search online for how to open files in your specific web browser.)

- Navigate to where you saved your new .xml file from Step 4 and double-click to open it. In my example, I'm using movies.xml.

You should now see your new data from your new fictional scenario. In my example, I see this:

| Movie Name | Starring Role | Box Office Sales |
|---|---|---|
| Love Story Number 3 | Julie Robertson | $265,000,099 |

## Congratulations!

You have written your first XML document and XSL stylesheet. At this point, you may be thinking: "Yeah, okay, but I didn't write it; I just changed what was already there." But here's a hint: Most coding starts off this way. It's rare for someone to sit down from scratch and write out, for instance, brand-new XML declarations and namespaces. Rather, they start off with some existing code and then make it their own.

In the next chapter, you'll create an XML document from scratch, using your own data.

# CHAPTER 3
# BUILDING OUT AN XML SINGLE-SOURCE DOCUMENT

## What You'll Learn

- What is an XML single-source document?
- What are they used for?
- How do you create one?

## What You'll Create

By the end of this chapter you will create a single-source XML document based on your own data.

## Required Tools and Supplies

You will need access to a good text editor, such as Notepad++, as well as access to at least one web browser. See Chapter 1 for download information.

# Starting Your Single-Source Project

In this section, I'll walk you through the steps toward completing a single-source document. Specifically, you'll build on the knowledge you learned in Chapter 2 and create two .xml files and two .xslt stylesheets —from scratch. In the end, you'll have two build-outs of information, each designed for a different rhetorical situation (audience, context, and purpose). They will each use the same data, but present it in different ways.

## Step 1: Determine Your Scenario

The first thing you must do is choose your scenario. That is, what type of data will you use to single-source? Will it be fictional? Or will it be something you actually use in the real world, such as information you could use at work? What you decide is up to you. The only guideline is you must have a decent amount of data to work with. **I recommend your project have *at least* 100 entries, with at least five categories**. (To compare, the XML you created in Chapter 2 just used one entry and three categories.)

In the examples that follow, I have chosen to use billing data for 100 patients from a fictional medical office.

## Step 2: Collect and Organize Your Data

I prefer to collect and organize data in a spreadsheet, but however you choose to collect and organize your data is up to you. See below for a few options for doing this; I'm sure there are more. (And, if you can come up with something else, you're welcome to use it.) The idea is to come up with a system that works for you, as you'll be inputting or copying/pasting in a bunch of data to populate your XML document.

## Option A: Type it By Hand

The first option is to type out your data by hand. This will involve a lot of copying and pasting into a text editor, but it's not undoable and is, in fact, a pretty good way to learn.

*Tip: For quicker copying and pasting on a PC, use Ctrl-C to copy text, and Ctrl-V to paste it.*

See the below example, where I've included the data on five different chiropractic patients. To reproduce this, I would highlight the text for one patient—starting with <patient> and ending with </patient>—and then copy it another 99 times. I'd then go back and change the data in between the start and end tags for <name>, <diagnosis_code>, <treatment>, <billing_code>, <billing_amount>, <insurance_company>, and <insurance_id> for each patient.

```
<chiropractic_office>
  <patient_data>
   <patient>
    <name>Darryl Bialaszewski</name>
     <diagnosis_code>739.0</diagnosis_code>
     <treatment>Adj</treatment>
     <billing_code>52103</billing_code>
     <billing_amount>58</billing_amount>
     <insurance_company>CIGNA</insurance_com
     pany>
     <insurance_id>7701782</insurance_id>
  </patient>
  <patient>
   <name>Tabatha Sloane</name>
     <diagnosis_code>739.1</diagnosis_code>
     <treatment>Micro</treatment>
     <billing_code>52104</billing_code>
     <billing_amount>88</billing_amount>
     <insurance_company>United
     Healthcare</insurance_company>
     <insurance_id>4864499</insurance_id>
  </patient>
  <patient>
    <name>Lonnie Baltzell</name>
     <diagnosis_code>739.2</diagnosis_code>
     <treatment>Adj+Micro</treatment>
     <billing_code>52105</billing_code>
     <billing_amount>108</billing_amount>
     <insurance_company>Safeco</insurance_co
     mpany>
     <insurance_id>1587308</insurance_id>
  </patient>
  <patient>
    <name>Chandra Ota</name>
     <diagnosis_code>739.3</diagnosis_code>
     <treatment>NP</treatment>
     <billing_code>52106</billing_code>
     <billing_amount>128</billing_amount>
     <insurance_company>State
```

```
    Farm</insurance_company>
    <insurance_id>4670219</insurance_id>
</patient>
<patient>
  <name>Allan Belli</name>
    <diagnosis_code>739.4</diagnosis_code>
    <treatment>NP+Micro</treatment>
    <billing_code>52107</billing_code>
    <billing_amount>148</billing_amount>
    <insurance_company>Progressive</insuran
    ce_company>
    <insurance_id>4109929</insurance_id>
</patient>
```

## Option B: Let a Spreadsheet Do the Work

If you're savvy with spreadsheets — or want to be — you can use an Excel spreadsheet or Google sheet to type and format your data. This involves creating a column for each code, another column for each data set, and then using formulas to put it all together. The end result isn't nearly as pretty, but gets the job done much more quickly, depending on how fast you type.

For this exercise, I used a Google Sheet to make the spreadsheet do the work for me. I input the data into columns, and then used the =CONCATENATE formula to bring it all together. (See this website for more information on how to use CONCATENATE to combine names in spreadsheets: https://edu.gcfglobal.org/en/excelformulas/using-concatenate-to-combine-names/1/.)

I also used the formula =CHAR(10) in some of the columns, which tells the computer to make a line break. (Here's a website that tells you how to use the CHAR function: https://exceljet.net/excel-functions/excel-char-function.)

# CODING FOR COMMUNICATORS

Once I got the formulas input and functional, I went back and copied and pasted the first column into my .xml file.

The resulting code looked like this for the first five patients:

```
<patient><name>Darryl Bialaszewski</name>
<diagnosis_code>739.0</diagnosis_code>
<treatment>Adj</treatment>
<billing_code>52103</billing_code>
<billing_amount>58</billing_amount>
<insurance_company>CIGNA</insurance_compan
y>
<insurance_id>7701782</insurance_id></pati
ent>
<patient><name>Tabatha Sloane</name>
<diagnosis_code>739.1</diagnosis_code>
<treatment>Micro</treatment>
<billing_code>52104</billing_code>
<billing_amount>88</billing_amount>
<insurance_company>United
Healthcare</insurance_company>
<insurance_id>4864499</insurance_id></pati
ent>
<patient><name>Lonnie Baltzell</name>
<diagnosis_code>739.2</diagnosis_code>
<treatment>Adj+Micro</treatment>
<billing_code>52105</billing_code>
<billing_amount>108</billing_amount>
<insurance_company>Safeco</insurance_compa
ny>
<insurance_id>1587308</insurance_id></pati
ent>
<patient><name>Chandra Ota</name>
<diagnosis_code>739.3</diagnosis_code>
<treatment>NP</treatment>
<billing_code>52106</billing_code>
<billing_amount>128</billing_amount>
<insurance_company>State
```

```
Farm</insurance_company>
<insurance_id>4670219</insurance_id></pati
ent>
<patient><name>Allan Belli</name>
<diagnosis_code>739.4</diagnosis_code>
<treatment>NP+Micro</treatment>
<billing_code>52107</billing_code>
<billing_amount>148</billing_amount>
<insurance_company>Progressive</insurance_
company>
<insurance_id>4109929</insurance_id></pati
ent>
```

I could have spent more time adding additional commands to create more line breaks, spacing, and so on—to make the code more readable and pretty, as in Option A—but I was short on time and wanted to rely on the computer to do the work for me.

Whichever option you choose is up to you. However, regardless of what you pick you'll need to put it into your XML files, which we'll start next.

> *Tip*: I used an online random name generator to come up with fictional names to use in my example. There are many similar sites that you can use to create the data you'll need for this project; simply do an online search to find them.

## Step 3: Create Your XML Documents

Here's where you'll start applying what you learned in Chapter 2, but in a much more sophisticated way.

- To begin, open up Notepad++ or your text editor of choice.

- Create a new document.

- Copy the below code:

```
<?xml version="1.0" encoding="ISO-
8859-1"?>
<?xml-stylesheet type="text/xsl"
href="chapter3_01.xslt"?>
```

- Save the document as chapter3_01.xml.

- Now, starting on the third line of code, start inputting your data that you collected in Step 2. For instance, mine would look like this:

```
<chiropractic_office>
  <patient_data>
    <patient>
      <name>Darryl Bialaszewski</name>
      <diagnosis_code>739.0</diagnosis_code>
      <treatment>Adj</treatment>
      <billing_code>52103</billing_code>
      <billing_amount>58</billing_amount>
      <insurance_company>CIGNA
      </insurance_company>
      <insurance_id>7701782</insurance_id>
        </patient>
```

- Fill in the information for all of your data sets; again, I recommend you have at least 100 unique entries with at least five categories. Above shows one entry (<patient>) with seven categories (<name>, <diagnosis_code>, <treatment>, <billing_code>, <billing_amount>, <insurance_company>, and <insurance_id>).

- When you're done inputting your data, be sure to close out the tags of your document. For instance, mine would close with:

```
</patient_data>
</chiropractic_office>
```

- Be sure to save your file.

## Step 4: Create Your Second XML File

Now, you'll do the same exact thing—but with a different named XSL stylesheet.

- Open up Notepad++ or your text editor of choice.

- Open up the file chapter3_01.xml you created in Step 3.

- Make a new copy of the .xml file, using one of these methods:

(1) Create a new text file. Copy the entire contents of chapter3_01.xml into that new file. Name it chapter3_02.xml and save it; OR

(2) Choose File --> Save As, and name it as chapter3_02.xml.

- On the second line of code, where you call out the .xslt file, rename the .xslt file to: chapter3_02.xslt, like this:

```
<?xml-stylesheet type="text/xsl"
href="level2_02.xslt"?>
```

- Save the file.

You should now have two separate .xml documents to work with. They should be identical, except for line two — where you call out two different XSL stylesheets.

## Step 5: Create Your XSL Stylesheets

- Once again, open up Notepad++ or your text editor of choice.

- Create a new file. Name it chapter3_01.xslt and save it in the same folder where you created your XML documents from above.

- In it, copy the below code:

```
<?xml version="1.0" encoding="ISO-8859-
1"?>
<xsl:stylesheet version="1.0"
xmlns:xsl="http://www.w3.org/1999/XSL/T
ransform">
<xsl:template match="/">
```

- Type in the code to transform format your XML data. Like in Chapter 2, we'll be using HTML so you can render your XML data in a web browser. To that end, you'll want to start with this code, beginning on line 4:

```
<table border="1" cellspacing="5"
cellpadding="5">
<tr>
<th>
```

Above, I've introduced a few new HTML callouts to help you display your data.

- **cellspacing** means that it creates additional spacing (in pixels) between the table cells. Here, cellspacing="5" means that it will add 5px (five pixels) of space between the cells.

- **cellpadding** means that it creates additional spacing (in pixels) between the walls of the cells and the content inside. Here, I've again used 5px for spacing.

- **tr** means a row inside of an HTML table.

- **th** means it's the header for a row inside of an HTML table.

Feel free to modify the border size, cellspacing, and cellpadding to your liking.

> *Note: Using border, cellspacing, and cellpadding callouts are no longer used in current forms of HTML5; however, this will work just fine for the learning you're doing in this book. You'll learn more about what to do with your code if using HTML5 and CSS starting in Chapter 5.*

- After the <th>—where the code indicates that you'll start the content for a new cell—it's time to input your table headings. For my example, I've used the following headings:

```
<th>Name</th>
  <th>Insurance ID</th>
  <th>Diagnosis Code</th>
  <th>Billing Code</th>
  <th>Billing Amount</th>
  <th>Insurance Company</th>
</tr>
```

Each cell will be a different table heading. Note that I remembered to end the table row with </tr> when I was done inputting my table headings.

- Next, use an XSL callout to tell the computer to pull data from each of your 100 entries. This is done by using the <xsl:for-each select=" "> tag. In my example, it looks like this:

```
<xsl:for-each
select="chiropractic_office/patient_dat
a/patient">
```

- Customize the above line in your own code by substituting the categories you've predefined in your XML datasheets.

- After that line, you can optionally tell the computer how you want the data sorted, such as by name, billing code, etc. In this example, I chose to sort it by insurance company name, so I have used the following code:

```
<xsl:sort select="insurance_company"/>
```

- Next, start a new row (using <tr>). Then tell the XSL sheet to format the information from each of your data tags, in your preferred order. Start and end each cell with <td> then use the XSL call out of

<xsl:value-of select=" "> to bring in the information from each data point. (By the way, **td** means the cell of the HTML table that holds the data.)

In the below example, I chose to do it in this order: name, insurance_id, diagnosis_code, billing_code, billing_amount, and insurance_company.

```
<tr>
   <td><xsl:value-of select="name"/></td>
   <td><xsl:value-of
select="insurance_id"/></td>
   <td><xsl:value-of
select="diagnosis_code"/></td>
   <td><xsl:value-of
select="billing_code"/></td>
   <td>$<xsl:value-of
select="billing_amount"/>.00</td>
   <td><xsl:value-of
select="insurance_company"/></td>
 </tr>
```

Note that for the "billing_amount" line I included a dollar sign ($) and a ".00" before and after the <xsl:value-of select="billing_amount"/> tag. This content will be "printed" before and after every single billing amount that shows up in my XML. That way, for the XML data itself, I only need to write (for instance) 58—but the XSL stylesheet will format and output it to say: $58.00. Feel free to add formatting touches such as this to your own XSLT stylesheets, as appropriate.

- Finally, remember to close all of your tags, including:

```
</xsl:for-each>
</table>
</xsl:template>
</xsl:stylesheet>
```

The end result for my XSL stylesheet looks like this in its entirety:

```
<?xml version="1.0" encoding="iso-8859-1"?>
<xsl:stylesheet
xmlns:xsl="http://www.w3.org/1999/XSL/Transf
orm" version="1.0">
<xsl:output method="html" />
<xsl:template match="/">
<table border="1" cellspacing="5"
cellpadding="5">
 <tr>
   <th>Name</th>
   <th>Insurance ID</th>
   <th>Diagnosis Code</th>
   <th>Billing Code</th>
   <th>Billing Amount</th>
   <th>Insurance Company</th>
  </tr>
 <xsl:for-each
select="chiropractic_office/patient_data/pat
ient">
<xsl:sort select="insurance_company"/>
  <tr>
    <td><xsl:value-of select="name"/></td>
    <td><xsl:value-of
```

```
select="insurance_id"/></td>
    <td><xsl:value-of
select="diagnosis_code"/></td>
    <td><xsl:value-of
select="billing_code"/></td>
    <td>$<xsl:value-of
select="billing_amount"/>.00</td>
    <td><xsl:value-of
select="insurance_company"/></td>
  </tr>
 </xsl:for-each>
</table>
</xsl:template>
</xsl:stylesheet>
```

- **Don't forget to save your work!** After you've done all of the above, click save. Make sure you've saved it in the same location (i.e., the same folder on your computer) as the chapter3_01.xml file you created previously in this chapter.

## Step 6: Create Your Second XSL Stylesheet

Same song, different verse. Now, you'll do the same exact thing—but with the data organized a bit differently. Here is where the single-sourcing really begins to get powerful.

- Open up Notepad++ or your text editor of choice.

- Open the file chapter3_01.xslt you created earlier.

- Make a new copy of the .xslt file, using one of these methods:

(1) Create a new text file. Copy and paste the entire contents of chapter3_01.xslt into that new file. Name it chapter3_02.xslt and save it; OR

(2) Choose File --> Save As, and name it chapter3_02.xslt.

- Modify and rearrange how you presented the data in the first XSL stylesheet so this one is *very different from the first and is intended for a different audience*.

For example, my first XSLT sheet was designed with the insurance company in mind, prioritizing the information that a billing company may prefer to see and in what order. This is why I had the information sorted by "insurance_company" and it included all of the codes and billing information.

It looked like this:

| Name | Insurance ID | Diagnosis Code | Billing Code | Billing Amount | Insurance Company |
|---|---|---|---|---|---|
| Tameka Newbern | 4293675 | 723.0 | 51028 | $58.00 | Blue Cross Blue Shield |
| Julio Ricketson | 6139668 | 724.9 | 52105 | $58.00 | Blue Cross Blue Shield |
| Max Wildes | 6395754 | 723.0 | 51027 | $108.00 | Blue Cross Blue Shield |
| Darren Mcquiggan | 4428277 | 724.9 | 52108 | $88.00 | Blue Cross Blue Shield |
| Nita Damiani | 3661963 | 723.0 | 52103 | $108.00 | Blue Cross Blue Shield |
| Amie Stellmacher | 7836506 | 724.9 | 51025 | $108.00 | Blue Cross Blue Shield |
| Lorrie Malagon | 5308388 | 723.0 | 52106 | $108.00 | Blue Cross Blue Shield |
| Hillary Mitten | 3448701 | 724.9 | 51028 | $128.00 | Blue Cross Blue Shield |
| Neil Buechler | 6437762 | 723.0 | 52109 | $128.00 | Blue Cross Blue Shield |
| Jami Lannon | 3007297 | 724.9 | 52104 | $148.00 | Blue Cross Blue Shield |
| Erik Brighton | 5930976 | 723.0 | 51026 | $128.00 | Blue Cross Blue Shield |
| Clayton Mccullah | 7314088 | 724.9 | 52107 | $58.00 | Blue Cross Blue Shield |
| Darryl Bialaszewski | 7701782 | 739.0 | 52103 | $58.00 | CIGNA |
| Pearlie Koren | 2302232 | 728.4 | 51025 | $108.00 | CIGNA |
| Penelope Glade | 4429923 | 739.0 | 52106 | $88.00 | CIGNA |
| Kelly Felch | 6184510 | 728.4 | 51028 | $108.00 | CIGNA |
| Rae Carriere | 6859353 | 739.0 | 52109 | $108.00 | CIGNA |
| Amie Quiros | 5302981 | 728.4 | 52104 | $108.00 | CIGNA |
| Nannie Pascoe | 4728598 | 739.0 | 51026 | $128.00 | CIGNA |
| Jamie Mccarville | 9053690 | 728.4 | 52107 | $128.00 | CIGNA |

However, now I want to create an XSL stylesheet designed for the *physician*, prioritizing the information *they* would want to see and in what order. In my fictional example, the doctor will be less concerned with the insurance information but more concerned with knowing the patients' names, treatments, and diagnoses.

# CODING FOR COMMUNICATORS

To that end, I changed my XSL stylesheet so the code looks like this:

```
<?xml version="1.0" encoding="iso-8859-1"?>
<xsl:stylesheet
xmlns:xsl="http://www.w3.org/1999/XSL/Transf
orm" version="1.0">
<xsl:output method="html" />
<xsl:template match="/">
<table border="1" cellspacing="5"
cellpadding="5">
 <tr>
   <th>Name</th>
   <th>Treatment</th>
   <th>Diagnosis Code</th>
   <th>Billing Amount</th>
  </tr>
<xsl:for-each
select="chiropractic_office/patient_data/pat
ient">
<xsl:sort select="name"/>
 <tr>
   <td><xsl:value-of select="name"/></td>
   <td><xsl:value-of
select="treatment"/></td>
   <td><xsl:value-of
select="diagnosis_code"/></td>
   <td>$<xsl:value-of
select="billing_amount"/>.00</td>
 </tr>
</xsl:for-each>
</table>
</xsl:template>
</xsl:stylesheet>
```

Note the key differences, including:

- o Sorting the information by name instead of insurance_company: `<xsl:sort select="name">`; and

- o Leaving out some of the information that the doctor may find irrelevant for their needs.

- Save the file. Again, make sure you've saved it in the same place on your computer as your other documents.

My example, which has now been formatted for a doctor's use, looks like this:

| Name | Insurance ID | Diagnosis Code | Billing Code | Billing Amount | Insurance Company |
|------|--------------|----------------|--------------|----------------|-------------------|
| Tameka Newbern | 4293675 | 723.0 | 51028 | $58.00 | Blue Cross Blue Shield |
| Julio Ricketson | 6139668 | 724.9 | 52105 | $58.00 | Blue Cross Blue Shield |
| Max Wildes | 6395754 | 723.0 | 51027 | $108.00 | Blue Cross Blue Shield |
| Darren Mcquiggan | 4428277 | 724.9 | 52108 | $88.00 | Blue Cross Blue Shield |
| Nita Damiani | 3661963 | 723.0 | 52103 | $108.00 | Blue Cross Blue Shield |
| Amie Stellmacher | 7836506 | 724.9 | 51025 | $108.00 | Blue Cross Blue Shield |
| Lorrie Malagon | 5308388 | 723.0 | 52106 | $108.00 | Blue Cross Blue Shield |
| Hillary Mitten | 3448701 | 724.9 | 51028 | $128.00 | Blue Cross Blue Shield |
| Neil Buechler | 6437762 | 723.0 | 52109 | $128.00 | Blue Cross Blue Shield |
| Jami Lannon | 3007297 | 724.9 | 52104 | $148.00 | Blue Cross Blue Shield |
| Erik Brighton | 5930976 | 723.0 | 51026 | $128.00 | Blue Cross Blue Shield |
| Clayton Mccullah | 7314088 | 724.9 | 52107 | $58.00 | Blue Cross Blue Shield |
| Darryl Bialaszewski | 7701782 | 739.0 | 52103 | $58.00 | CIGNA |
| Pearlie Koren | 2302232 | 728.4 | 51025 | $108.00 | CIGNA |
| Penelope Glade | 4429923 | 739.0 | 52106 | $88.00 | CIGNA |
| Kelly Felch | 6184510 | 728.4 | 51028 | $108.00 | CIGNA |
| Rae Carriere | 6859353 | 739.0 | 52109 | $108.00 | CIGNA |
| Amie Quiros | 5302981 | 728.4 | 52104 | $108.00 | CIGNA |
| Nannie Pascoe | 4728598 | 739.0 | 51026 | $128.00 | CIGNA |
| Jamie Mccarville | 9053690 | 728.4 | 52107 | $128.00 | CIGNA |

## Hooray!

You have now completed your first single-sourced XML project and know enough about XML and XSL to be dangerous. For most beginners, this is likely all you need to know to have a basic understanding of XML. However, if you want to take your skills to the next level, in the next chapter you'll learn how to master more sophisticated software.

# CHAPTER 4
# MASTERING XML EDITING
# SOFTWARE

## What You'll Learn

- How to transform and format XML in multiple additional ways.
- How to use a top XML software package to create technical documents and present XML data in additional formats (e.g., HTML and PDF).

## What You'll Create

By the end of this chapter you will feel comfortable with at least one of the leading XML software packages, and will single-source at least one major document.

## Required Tools and Supplies

You will need access to a good text editor, such as Notepad++, as well as access to at least one web browser and at least one XML Editor. You'll also need at least a trial version of one of the leading software packages: either MadCap Flare or Adobe Framemaker. See Chapter 1 for download information.

## Why Keep Going with XML?

So far, you've learned enough about XML to get by in just about any professional technical communication setting. However, many technical communicators use large and expensive software packages to write and edit their XML and single-source documents in various, more complex ways.

Some people (like me) think the practice is (mostly) unnecessary. For instance, I enjoy writing directly into a text editor and manipulating the code directly. However, some people don't want to bother with code at all and would rather learn complex software to do the work for them. Plus, the software often has vast capabilities—such as moving beyond HTML outputs—that will save you tons of time and work.

My hope is by the end of this chapter you will have learned the best of both worlds. That is, in previous chapters you learned enough coding to get your feet wet and understand what happens behind the scenes.

In this chapter you'll progress to understanding how to apply this knowledge within an expansive software program that will extend the capabilities of what you can do with XML.

## What You'll Do in This Chapter

For this chapter, you will dive into a software package of your choice, learn the basics, and then single source some XML documents in HTML and PDF.

To begin, choose one of the software packages below and follow the instructions. You will:

(1) Download and learn the basics of the software.
(2) Follow along with some tutorials, linked below.
(3) Create some deliverables, as outlined below, to demonstrate your mastery of the software and associated XML concepts.

## Step 1: Choose Your Software

First, you need to choose a software package to work with. The options are below, ordered by my recommendations — although you're welcome to try whichever you like. Both are excellent choices for adding to your resume; they are the most commonly used XML software packages used in industry:

> **MadCap Flare**: This is a professional software package used by many professional technical writers. Start here, if you can. However, they only have a free 30-day trial.
>
> **Recommended for**: People who like learning through videos and webinars. Available at: https://madcapsoftware.com.

**Adobe FrameMaker**: An alternative to MadCap Flare, Adobe FrameMaker does have a free trial as well.

**Recommended for**: Adobe evangelists; if you already know and like Adobe's other products, you may like and prefer this one, too. Also a good choice, like MadCap Flare, for people who like and prefer video tutorials. Available at: https://www.adobe.com/products/framemaker.html.

*BONUS CHALLENGE! For an extra learning opportunity, try both—and follow along for the rest of this chapter using both software packages.*

## Step 2: Learn the Ropes

Now that you've chosen a software package to try, now it's time to run through some tutorials until you're comfortable with it. Of course, you're welcome to just dive in and try to learn it on your own, but in my experience these tutorials will be invaluable to you; I'd suggest at least starting with them.

*Note: If you're still not sure which XML editing software you prefer, I recommend browsing through the below information for both software packages until you see a tutorial style that appeals to you the most.*

## Option A: MadCap Flare

MadCap Flare has introductory documentation available in either PDF or video format. This could be a good choice if you like having printed documentation, but also enjoy videos (as they have many videos on their website). If you've chosen to work with MadCap Flare, complete the following for this part of the exercise:

> Read/browse through Chapters 1 and 2 of the MadCap Flare Getting Started Guide at: https://docs.madcapsoftware.com/flare2020/Flare-Getting-Started-Guide.pdf.

> Work through the introductory Getting Started Tutorial for MadCap Flare (found by opening up the software itself).

> Watch the Getting Started with MadCap Flare video, which is hosted on their website, here: https://www.madcapsoftware.com/videos/flare/.

*Note: If you're using an older or newer version of MadCap Flare, you can access the most recent versions of their Getting Started Guides here: https://www.madcapsoftware.com/products/flare/getting-started/.*

## Option B: Adobe FrameMaker

If you're already familiar with Adobe products, then FrameMaker may seem somewhat familiar to you, even right out of the box. However, you may also know that Adobe products are renowned for being a bit difficult to learn, at least at first. If FrameMaker is your choice of software for this chapter, then look through the following:

Getting Started with Adobe FrameMaker (available here in either HTML or PDF versions: https://help.adobe.com/en_US/framemaker/2019/using/index .html), including the following sections:
- What is FrameMaker
    - Author and enrich content
    - Manage and collaborate
    - Publish across multiple channels
    - Supported software
- Authoring Modes
    - FrameMaker mode
    - Structured FrameMaker mode
    - Choose an authoring mode

*Note: If you are using an older or newer version of Adobe FrameMaker, you can download all of their tutorials in Print or HTML format here: https://helpx.adobe.com/framemaker/archive.html.*

## Step 3: Prepare Your XML Document

Now that you've selected a software program and have learned a bit about the basics of using it, it's time to prepare an XML document to use for creating your project.

### Open Your XML Document

The file you will start with to work on the below project is the final .xml file you worked on in Chapter 3. (I recommend using chapter3_01.xml, but you may use that or chapter3_02.xml.) Open it up now in your text editor of choice.

### Add Some New Data

Now add at least one more data point that includes writing in paragraph format. As an example, I might add to a data point that discusses the patient's medical history, like this (the content I've added is in **bold**; no need to bold it yourself while completing this exercise):

```
<chiropractic_office>
  <patient_data>
    <patient>
      <name>Darryl Bialaszewski</name>
      <diagnosis_code>739.0</diagnosis_code>
      <treatment>Adj</treatment>
      <billing_code>52103</billing_code>
      <billing_amount>58</billing_amount>
      <insurance_company>CIGNA
      </insurance_company>
      <insurance_id>7701782</insurance_id>
      <medical_history>Mr. Bialaszewski is
```

```
    51-years old. He has seen a
    chiropractor for the past 17 years,
    mostly for sciatica. He has a family
    medical history that includes heart
    disease and diabetes. His primary
    issues now include back pain, neck
    tension, and stress related to his
    career.</medical_history>
  </patient>
```

For this exercise, add at least a paragraph (2-3 sentences) of written data for each of your data points. In my medical file example, I would add a paragraph of <medical_history> for all 100 patient files.

*Note: While you're welcome to write new content for each, feel free to copy and paste some around so that you have 100 paragraphs but some of them repeat. That is, you don't have to write 100 new paragraphs—unless, of course, the data is existing or you really want to. (If you really want to get into it, you can find online backstory generators, like this one, that will generate content for you.) The idea, of course, is simply to practice with the software and get more comfortable with larger XML data sets.*

**Save It**

I suggest saving it as a new file named chapter4.xml.

# Step 4: Single-Source Your XML Content

So, you've chosen a software program and prepared your XML document. Now you can create your deliverables. See below for instructions on what you'll complete to practice your new skills. In all cases, you'll learn how to move beyond XSLT stylesheets and use a robust software program to output your XML in multiple formats; in this case: HTML and PDF.

**Option A: MadCap Flare**

To complete this option, follow the below steps:

**Read, Watch, and Learn More About Single-Source Authoring in MadCap Flare (Optional)**

This part is optional, but you may want to start by learning more about single-source authoring and what you can do with MadCap Flare. If so, check out:

> This short article about the power of single-sourcing content in MadCap Flare:
> https://www.madcapsoftware.com/blog/single-sourcing-explained-the-power-of-madcap-flare/;
> and/or

> The following webinar: "An Overview of MadCap Flare: Topic-Based Authoring and Single-Source Publishing" (1 hour, 7 minutes):
> https://www.madcapsoftware.com/webinars/an-overview-madcap-flare-topic-based-authoring-single-sourcing.

### Learn How to Add Topics and Other Elements in MadCap Flare

Open the Flare Getting Started Guide (previously downloaded                                         here: https://docs.madcapsoftware.com/flare2020/Flare-Getting-Started-Guide.pdf) and read Chapters 3 and 4. You'll need this information in Steps 3 and 4, when you're creating and modifying your XML file.

### Open or Create Your Starting XML Project

Launch MadCap Flare. Then, follow the instructions in Chapter 2 of the Flare Getting Started Guide, on how to create a new project.

You may choose an existing template or a custom template, should you prefer to create one yourself. Your goal will be to create a version of your document that is in HTML, XML, and PDF versions. That is, you will create three documents that have been created from the same single-source.

> *Note: A project is a collection of XML and other files; start with the chapter4.xml document as the first element of your project. Also use that file if you need to add any additional information by hand.*

### Modify Your XML Project

Next, you'll modify your XML project to include some of the features in MadCap Flare. This is how you'll demonstrate your mastery of the content in this chapter. To do so, open your chapter4.xml file in MadCap Flare (or start a new document and copy and paste in your content as needed). Save it as something new so you don't lose your work; I recommend something like chapter4_02.xml.

Then, follow the instructions in Chapter 3 of the Flare Getting Started Guide and add the following elements to your XML file, referring back to the MadCap Flare documentation, as necessary:

- Create at least three **topics**.

- Use at least one **cross-reference**.

*Note: Although you can use any XML content to use as a cross-reference, I recommend using chapter3_02.xml from the previous chapter as your secondary XML document. Then, you can link to it using the cross-reference function. Your goal is to determine if you understand how cross-referencing works and how to do it.*

- Write at least one **footnote**, to be used as part of a PDF output.

- Incorporate at least one **image** to be included in your final documents (both HTML and PDF).

- Use at least three **variables**—either pre-defined or those you create yourself.

- Choose at least one of the following additional features to include:

  o A **glossary** of at least two terms your users may need to know.

  o A **multimedia** content element, such as a video or audio file.

  o A **page layout** to define headers, footers, and more for a print-based (e.g., PDF) file.

  o A **QR code** that links to additional content.

  o A **slideshow** to incorporate multiple forms of content into one file.

  o A **table** to present data and other information useful for your readers.

  o An interactive **table of contents**.

Instructions for all of the aforementioned features may be found in the Flare Getting Started Guide, Chapter 3. You may find additional resources in the MadCap Knowledge Base, at: https://kb.madcapsoftware.com/Content/Welcome.htm.

**Learn About Targets and Outputs**

Starting in Chapter 5 of the Getting Started Guide, you'll learn about outputting your work into digital and print formats. Specifically, read about how to create an output in HTML and PDF.

- Link to the HTML5 guide is here: https://docs.madcapsoftware.com/flare2020r3/Flare-HTML5-Guide.pdf.

- Link to the Print guide is here: https://docs.madcapsoftware.com/flare2020r3/Flare-Printed-Output-Guide.pdf.

Each links to another series of complex information that teaches you how to output in either HTML5 or print. Because each are complex enough tasks in and of themselves, for the purposes of this project, you'll focus on the latter: print.

To use a print-based output, Flare uses a concept called targets, which you create to give the software instructions on how to output and format your XML—such as outputting to PDF or to a Word document.

Access the Printed Output Guide for Flare (found at: https://docs.madcapsoftware.com/flare2020r3/Flare-Printed-Output-Guide.pdf). Read at least Chapter 8, which is where you'll learn about targets and outputs. Then, do the following:

- Make sure you have some **targets** in your document. The chapter walks you through how to modify or add a target to your project.

- Create at least two **condition tags**. Imagine you'll create two different PDF files—much like you created two different XSLT stylesheets previously in this book. That is, you want to print two PDFs from the same information for the purposes of two different rhetorical situations; i.e., you want to single-source.

Imagine that you'll be giving each PDF to a separate audience.

- Next, read about **print-based PDF outputs**. This is what you'll be working on. Chapter 8 tells you how to change an output type for your target(s); make sure you select PDF.

- Then, output your XML into PDF. Once again, see the Flare Getting Started Guide or the MadCap Knowledge Base for additional help and information.

## Option B: Adobe FrameMaker

To complete this option, follow the below steps:

### Read the Complete Online Tutorial for Single-Sourcing XML Content in Adobe FrameMaker

Browse through the entire tutorial found on this site (https://help.adobe.com/en_US/framemaker/2019/using/index.html) entitled "Single-sourcing content," including:
- Conditional text (and all associated sub-links);
- Cross-references (and all associated sub-links);
- Text insets (and all associated sub-links); and
- Variables (and all associated sub-links).

You will need to know all of the above for creating your deliverables.

## Open or Create Your Starting XML Document

Launch Adobe FrameMaker. Then, follow the instructions here, on how to create a document: https://help.adobe.com/en_US/framemaker/2019/ using/index.html; click on: FrameMaker Basics → Documents → Create a Document.

You may choose an existing template or a custom template, should you prefer to create one yourself. Your goal will be to create a version of your document that is in HTML, XML, and PDF versions. That is, you will create three documents that have been created from the same single-source.

The starting document you'll need to complete this project is the chapter4.xml document you saved earlier in this chapter. Open it in FrameMaker, or copy and paste it into FrameMaker as a new XML document.

## Modify Your XML Document Using the FrameMaker Functions You've Learned

Now, that you have an XML file to start with, modify it using the FrameMaker functions you read about earlier in the tutorial.

Although the form of the edits you make will vary depending on the topic of your XML file, there are some things to consider in terms of mastering FrameMaker.

Specifically, you should be able to do the following:

- Use both conditional and unconditional text, with a minimum of three **conditional tags** that change depending on the format of your output (e.g., HTML or PDF).

- Use at least one **cross-reference**. Your goal is to demonstrate that you understand how cross-referencing works and how to do it.

- Include at least one **text inset**. See this link on how to insert text insets; this might be from a Word Doc, a PDF, or a text file.

- Use at least three **variables**—either pre-defined or those you create yourself.

- Incorporate at least one **graphic or visual** in your final documents (both HTML and PDF).

**Save Your Work so that it Single-Sources in both HTML and PDF Formats**

Save your document in all three formats listed: HTML, XML, and PDF. (You will need to save it three separate times, one for each format.) See the tutorial here under FrameMaker Basics → Documents → Save a Document: https://help.adobe.com/en_US/framemaker/2019/using/index.html.

## Congratulations!

You have learned new coding techniques and have begun to master the most common tools and technologies for XML and XSL. If you had trouble with this section, don't worry. The content in this chapter is supposed to be difficult. You may have several learning curves and moments of frustrations and confusion along the way. This is to be expected, as part of the growing pains of learning new skills, tools, and technologies.

However, each of us have different strengths, abilities, and learning styles. So, if you start this (or any) project and don't finish all the way, I'd suggest reflecting a bit on your learning process. My favorite tool for this is journaling. I always find it helpful to sit down and briefly write about my process, what I learned, and what I feel like I'm struggling with. This gives me perspective on how far I've come rather than focus on elements that maybe were too difficult or presented stumbling blocks.

If this happens to you, I recommend trying to journal and then let this sit for a few days before coming back to it. Trying again with fresh eyes is a wonderful technique for learning any new topic—especially when it comes to new technologies.

In the next chapter, we'll build on what you've learned with XML and dive into web development, utilizing basic skills in HTML and CSS.

# CHAPTER 5
# INTRODUCTION TO
# HTML5 AND CSS3

## What You'll Learn

- What is HTML5 and CSS3?
- How does HTML5 and CSS3 work and how are the documents structured?
- How do you get started coding with HTML5 and CSS3?

## What You'll Create

By the end of this chapter, you will have coded your first pages of HTML5 and CSS3.

## Required Tools and Supplies

You will need access to a good text editor, such as Notepad++, as well as access to at least one web browser. See Chapter 1 for download information.

You will also need some various online reference guides, which I'll link to throughout the chapters that follow.

## Optional Tools and Supplies

Although it's not required, you may want to have an additional book or handbook at your side, depending on your learning style. Here are a few of my favorites:

### *HTML and CSS* by Jon Duckett

> **Why you'd want it**: This is a great book for traditional learners who like a combination of visuals, text, and hands-on examples for learning. It would be a good choice if you want a backup text that will provide clear examples, and also can be used as a reference. I also recommend this if you want to continue with HTML and CSS beyond this book, as it provides an excellent beginning-to-intermediate foundation that will serve you well if you intend to continue learning about coding. Available at Amazon.com and other retailers.

### *Build Your Own Website: A Comic Guide to HTML, CSS, and WordPress* by Nate Cooper with Art by Kim Gee

> **Why you'd want it**: If you are almost primarily a visual learner, and also like the structure of comics, you might really enjoy this illustrated guide to coding in HTML and CSS. It's also a good choice if you're intimidated by HTML/CSS or aren't sure you're quite getting the concepts. Finally, it's a good primer if you're interested in learning WordPress (something we won't cover in this book). Available at

Amazon.com and other retailers.

## What is HTML?

Hypertext Markup Language—or HTML for short—is a markup language used to create digital deliverables, such as websites and apps. It is used primarily for **structure** and **organization** of web documents.

## What is a Markup Language?

As discussed in Chapter 2, a markup language is a coding language used primarily for the web. It consists of rules and tags (more on this later), and is a way of categorizing, processing, and presenting information. Examples of markup languages you may have heard of include XML, XHTML, and HTML.

## A Brief History of HTML

Sir Tim Berners-Lee—widely known as the inventor of the Internet—created HTML in 1990. There were three major parts to his invention, which remain cornerstones to the Internet as we know it today:

**HTML: Hypertext Markup Language**—which allows for us to format and write content for the Internet.

**URI/URL: Uniform Resource Identifier/Uniform Resource Locator**—commonly called URLs and otherwise known as web addresses.

For instance, http://google.com is a URL; it's a web address you type into your web browser to visit the Google search engine.

**HTTP: Hypertext Transfer Protocol**—this is what you see at the beginning of URLs and it's what allows the computer to retrieve or transfer content from across the Internet.

*Note: You may also see HTTPS (Secure Hypertext Transfer Protocol); secure protocols are used on sites where you provide confidential information such as credit card numbers or passwords. For example: https://amazon.com.*

*You've probably also noticed that you don't need to type in http:// or https:// for your web browser to find the website you'd like to visit; your browser will automatically populate the appropriate protocol. For instance, if you type "buzzfeed.com" into your web browser, it will bring you to Buzzfeed's home page, which is at this URL: https://buzzfeed.com.*

If you're as old as I am, you may also remember the term WWW or the World Wide Web. This was Berners-Lee's first invention, the first iteration of the Internet as we now know it. It used to be that you had to enter "www" before a web address, such as: www.google.com. This is no longer true and is in fact no longer recommended. If you're curious to learn more about why we no longer use "www" in web addresses, see this article: https://dropwww.com/why.

Since Berners-Lee's first iteration of HTML in 1990, we've had five more iterations, as well as an offshoot called XHTML. XHTML was created in 2000 as a way to extend HTML to further capabilities (hence the acronym XHTML, which stands for eXtensible Hypertext Markup Language). You can think of it as a bit like XML and HTML blended together.

In 2008, they released HTML5 (credited to developer Ian Hickson), which was the fifth iteration of HTML and a further extension of the capabilities of the coding technology. It also made XHTML nearly obsolete, as HTML5 can do nearly all the things that XHTML is capable of. In the end, they are all very closely related; HTML5 is very close to HTML, with a few changes that help with accessibility and usability. It also helps you code more quickly and efficiently. (To learn more about the history of HTML5, visit this website to read a short article and an infographic on the topic: https://mashable.com/2012/07/17/history-html5/#bchE03rJHsqW.)

With that said, in this book you'll learn HTML5—which is the latest and greatest standard in web development coding. However, note that I'm old and first learned HTML in the 1990s, so I often use the terms HTML and HTML5 interchangeably.

## How Does HTML Work?

Much like XML, HTML uses tags to organize and construct its content. The difference is while XML is extensible and therefore customizable, HTML uses specific tags to structure and organize its information. In some ways, it makes learning HTML easier than XML, because you can look up any tags you need to do the specific functions you're trying to accomplish.

Back up. What is a tag?

A tag is a way of structuring and organizing content. Just like XML, in HTML there are two types of tags:

The **start tag,** which looks like this: <tag>

The **end tag,** which includes a forward slash, like this: </tag>

Tags are used to categorize your content. You might think of them as labels. The primary content of what you're writing goes between the opening tag and the closing tag.

Note that every **start tag** must also have an **end tag,** to indicate to the computer where the associated information starts and stops. Whatever content you place between the start tag and the end tag is what will be defined by the document as the content for that tag.

Unlike XML, however, you can't just put whatever you want into HTML tags. HTML tags are **predefined**, meaning they're defined for you and each one has its own meaning. In this project you'll learn many of the common HTML5 tags, so you'll learn the basics as we go.

## Example of an HTML5 Tag

Here's one of the most common HTML5 tags: <p>— which stands for paragraph. To write this sentence in HTML5, I'd put it in tags, like this:

```
<p>To write this sentence in HTML5, I'd
put it in tags, like this.</p>
```

The content between the start <p> tag and the end </p> tag is what is included in the paragraph. If I added a second paragraph, it would look like this:

```
<p>To write this sentence in HTML5,
I'd put it in tags, like this.</p>
<p>Now I want to create a second
paragraph so I'll type it within new
tags, like this.</p>
```

Starting a new <p> tag will tell the computer to make a line break (put a space between paragraphs). Unlike in print document production, it's not easy to indent text. Therefore, almost all text on the web is left-aligned with paragraph line breaks between paragraphs.

## What You Can (and Can't) Do with HTML5

**Some things you can do with HTML5:**

- Write and edit website content.
- Organize your content with headings and subheadings.
- Create bulleted and numbered lists.
- Create tables and forms.
- Create descriptive hyperlinks.
- Embed multimedia elements, such as video and audio.
- Make content accessible, including providing screen readers with descriptive text for images and hyperlinks, and creating accessible forms and buttons.
- Create websites that are responsive, meaning that they work on various sizes of screens—both on computers and on mobile devices.

**What you can't do with HTML5:**

- Design or style your content.

It used to be that you'd use HTML to do just about anything in web development—including the design of the website itself. Current standards for HTML5, however, recommend using CSS for all design elements of website development. So, while you technically can do web design in HTML, you really shouldn't. For the purposes of this book, one thing you can't do with HTML5 is design anything. Elements such as colors, fonts, and alignments—everything you learn in traditional print document design, including Robin Patricia Williams's CRAP design principles (contrast, repetition, alignment, and proximity)—are done instead in CSS.

 *Note: Robin Patricia Williams's classic book* **The Non-Designer's Design Book** *is worth reading, if you haven't read it already.*

## Okay... But What Is CSS?

CSS is short for Cascading Style Sheet, and it's used to add visual design to your webpages. In Chapters 2-4 you learned about using XSL (eXtensible Stylesheet Language) as a way of formatting and transforming your XML. CSS is the web version of that; it's a style sheet that is used to transform and format your HTML code.

Of course, developers can't make anything easy—so like HTML vs. HTML5, there is also a new name for the latest CSS: it's called CSS3. Again, what you'll be learning in this book is CSS3, but I'll often refer to it as CSS, for the sake of simplicity. If you want to read about the technical differences between CSS and CSS3, click here.

From a practical standpoint, though, the differences between HTML/HTML5 and CSS/CSS3 don't matter much outside of professional web development—but it will sound fancier to insiders if you put HTML5 and CSS3 on your resume instead of HTML and CSS. It will indicate for your readers that you're familiar with the latest standards in web coding.

## How Does CSS Work?

Much like the relationship between XML and XSLT, HTML and CSS work hand-in-hand. You write up your code for all of your written and multimedia content in HTML5. Then, you write a separate document that defines all of the styling— fonts, colors, sizes, headings, spacing, alignment, and so on— in a CSS3 file. You refer to this CSS3 file in your HTML5 document, so that the computer knows where to look up how to style your webpage.

## Why Does This Matter?

Back in the day, developers would use HTML (and a bit of JavaScript) for everything. This meant that if you wanted to change the spacing of a sidebar or the size of a font on a website, you had to open up every single HTML page and edit it with the new information. CSS makes it so you can change the entire website's font, colors, layout, and so on in just one place. It's pretty powerful and is a huge time-saver. Plus, it's fairly slick and easy to learn. I'll prove it next, when you'll finally get your hands on some code.

# Rules for Getting Started with HTML5 and CSS3

Before we do anything else, there are a few rules you should know about getting started. Because HTML5 and CSS are hierarchical languages, it's important that you follow some very basic rules for naming, creating, and storing files. Some of these are hard and fast rules and others are pointers I've picked up over the years. I suggest using all of them for now.

Take time to **prepare your workspace**. Before you get started on any web coding project, open Windows Explorer (for PC users) or Finder (for Mac users) and create the following folder hierarchy:

**Primary project folder**: This can be named anything you like, so long as it only uses lowercase letters, numbers, underscores, or hyphens. Make it as short and as descriptive as possible; for instance: codeproject01. This folder is where you will keep all of your .html files for your project. Inside your primary project folder, create two additional folders:

- css
- media

*Note*: *They should be named this exactly, using lowercase letters. These folders are where you will house your .css files and your multimedia content (such as images and videos), respectively.*

Always save HTML files with the **.html** extension, and always save CSS files with the **.css** extension.

Always name the HTML file for the homepage of your website **index.html**, and always name the primary CSS file for your website **main.css**.

**Do not use any special characters** in your file names. Only use letters (a-z) and numbers (0-9).

**Never use spaces** in file names or in any of your code. When naming files, if you must separate multiple words you can use underscores (_) or hyphens (-) instead.

**Use only lowercase** letters when naming HTML or CSS files.

**Don't start the names of your files with numbers**; start with letters instead. For instance, you may name it test01.html but not 01test.html.

**Keep names of files short and sweet**. Never go beyond 4 or 5 words, and try to be much shorter than that. Remember, some people still type in URLs from scratch when visiting websites, and every space or character you use will be another keystroke.

At the same time, **try and be as descriptive as possible with your naming conventions** (with the exception of your two primary files: index.html and main.css). For example, something like contact.html is a much better name for a Contact Us page than form.html.

Always **pay attention to where you're saving files and how you're naming them**. This may seem silly at first, but the larger the site the more pages you'll have to keep track of and organize. It's best to get into a good habit now of knowing what you're saving and where.

Okay, now let's get to work.

## Structuring HTML and CSS

To create an HTML page, you start by opening up a text file in Notepad++ or your text editor of choice and then typing in a callout, to tell the computer what format to expect.

In HTML5, the first line of every HTML page should start with this:

```
<!DOCTYPE html>
```

# CODING FOR COMMUNICATORS

A short, basic HTML page might therefore look like this:

```
<!DOCTYPE html>
<html>
  <head>
    <title>My Personal Website</title>
  </head>
  <body>
    <p>This is my first basic HTML
page!</p>
  </body>
</html>
```

Note that in the above example, I used the **<html>** tag to start the document; like the <!DOCTYPE html> first line, that is required in all HTML pages.

After that, I used the **<head>** tag, which indicates the heading portion of the HTML page. This often includes the page title—indicated here with the **<title>** tag— which is the text that shows up on the tab of your browser when you're looking at a website. (Note it's between the <head> start tag and the </head> end tag.) Remember to always choose a descriptive title for your website that will tell your users what to expect from your page.

Next, I used the **<body>** tag, to tell the computer where the header information ends and the body of text begins.

Embedded within the <body> tag I also used the <p> tag to start a new paragraph.

Then, I remembered to end the </body> and </html> tags. This last part is important: every start tag also needs an end tag. You can also see in the above example how the structure of HTML is embedded. That is, it remains in order—and it opens and closes in the same order hierarchically from one another.

The first part of learning HTML5 is really understanding how the language works—and remembering that **organization, hierarchy, and details matter**. Once you've got that down, HTML5 is arguably the easiest coding language to learn. It's intuitive and because the information is structured and hierarchical it also works nicely with a technical communication mindset—which is focused on clear, concise language organized in a logical, usable way.

The rest, if I'm being honest, is all stuff you can look up in a reference book (such as remembering a particular tag or how to structure a certain look or layout you're trying to achieve). By the end of this book, you'll learn how to leverage available resources to create and/or modify your own websites using HTML5 and CSS3.

## Your First HTML5 Web Page

Now it's time for you to try for yourself what you saw in action above. Follow these steps:

- Create your workspace, as described in the rules at the beginning of this chapter. For my example, I'll open up Windows Explorer and create a folder called codingproject01. Inside, I'll create two more folders: (1) css; and (2) media.

- Now, open up Notepad++ or your text editor of choice.

- Create a new document.

- Copy the following code into the text file:

```
<!DOCTYPE html>
<html>
  <head>
    <title>My Personal Website</title>
  </head>
  <body>
    <p>This is my first basic HTML
page!</p>
  </body>
</html>
```

- Save it as **index.html**—and make sure you save it inside of your primary project folder. (In this case, I've put everything in my folder called "codingproject01" so I can easily find it later.) My folder and file hierarchy now looks like this in Windows Explorer:

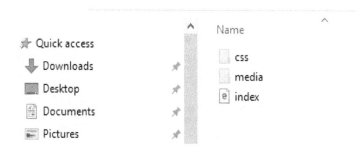

- Next, open up your web browser of choice. In your browser, use Ctrl-O—which is the command to open a local file. Navigate to your primary project folder. Double-click the index.html file or click it and select "Open."

Now you should be able to view your first HTML5 page! It probably looks something like this:

This is my first basic HTML page!

Note that this first attempt doesn't look fancy. In fact, it should look like basic black font (it probably looks like Times New Roman) on a white background. That's okay, because you'll add the style later with CSS3. In fact, let's try it now.

## Your First CSS3 Style Sheet

- Go back to Notepad++ or your text editor of choice.

- Create another new document.

- Copy the following code into the text file:

```
body
{
background-color: #D9BEE7;
}
p
{
font-family: Helvetica, Arial, sans-
serif;
font-size: 2em;
}
```

 *Important Note: Be sure you're paying attention to spacing, capitalization, and punctuation.*

Keep everything lowercase. Make spaces where there needs to be spaces; use colons, hyphens, semicolons, etc. *exactly* as it shows above.

- Using the command "File --> Save As" (or whatever command your text editor uses to save a document), save the file you created **inside the css folder**. (This is the folder you created inside your primary project folder, as part of setting up your workspace.) Name the file main.css.

- Now go back to Notepad++ or your text editor of choice and reopen index.html. Modify the code so that it looks like this (the part in **bold** is the part I added; no need to bold it on your computer):

```
<!DOCTYPE html>
<html>
  <head>
    <title>My Personal Website</title>
    <link rel="stylesheet"
type="text/css" href="css/main.css" />
  </head>
  <body>
    <p>This is my first basic HTML
page!</p>
  </body>
</html>
```

- Click "Save."

- Finally, go back to your web browser and use Ctrl-O to open **index.html**. If you still have it open from above, press the F5 command or select the refresh button on your web browser (to the left of the URL) to refresh the page. You should now see something like this:

# This is my first basic HTML page!

Hooray! Now you're on your way to learning to style and format your pages with CSS3. Let's break it down so you can see how it's done.

## Reading the <link> Tag in HTML5

The code you just added to your index.html file is what's called the **<link>** tag. It tells the computer to link to the CSS file and then use the instructions you've written in the CSS to format the HTML.

Let's look at it again:

```
<link rel="stylesheet" type="text/css"
href="css/main.css" />
```

Within the <link> tag there are three properties and three values:

**rel="stylesheet"**: "rel" stands for relationship and specifies the relationship between the HTML document and whatever you're linking. In this case, you're linking to a CSS file, which is a stylesheet. Therefore, the relationship to the <link> is that it's a stylesheet.

**type="text/css"**: this part tells the computer what type of stylesheet you're using. In this case, you're specifying that it's a text-based CSS file.

**href="css/main.css"**: "href" is short for hypertext reference; this final part gives the URL of where the computer can find the actual stylesheet. This is veryimportant; it specifies the specific location of the CSS file. In this case, you're saying it's in the "css" folder and it's called "main.css."

> *Note: Be sure to notice the ending portion of the tag has a space before the forward slash. This is something you'll see frequently in HTML5, so make sure you keep an eye out for adding appropriate spaces when necessary.*

## Reading the CSS3 Code

```
body
{
background-color: #D9BEE7;
}
p
{
font-family: Helvetica, Arial, sans-
serif;
font-size: 2em;
}
```

Just like HTML5, CSS3 is a hierarchical language, meaning the order of elements matters. Also, the order of the CSS3 properties you include should mimic the order of the HTML5 tags you've written.

If you put the <body> tag first in HTML5 (as you should) followed by the <p> tag to create a new paragraph, then the CSS3 document should also start by calling out what to do with the "body" and then the "p" of the content.

⚠ *Important Note: When in doubt, mimic the* **exact** *order you've used for your HTML5 code.* **The order matters.** *This will become even more important later in this book as you add more and more tags to your HTML5 files.*

The difference between HTML5 and CSS3 is that CSS doesn't have start tags and end tags. Instead, CSS uses what are called **selectors**, **declarations**, **properties**, and **values**. Let's break it down.

**Selectors** are what CSS3 uses to select a certain amount of content in the HTML5 code. These are the parts of the CSS that come before the opening curly cue brackets ( { ). In the above code, our selectors are body and p.

**Declarations** are what we're declaring that we want our HTML5 code to look like.
The content between the curly brackets ( { ) and ( } ) is what is called a declaration block. Curly brackets are aligned on a line all by themselves. For example, the following four lines of CSS code is a declaration block:

```
{
font-family: Helvetica, Arial,
sans-serif;
font-size: 2em;
}
```

Each line of code that ends with a semicolon ( ; ) is an individual **declaration**. In our main.css file, for instance, we have three declarations (background-color, font-family, and font-size):

```
background-color: #D9BEE7

font-family: Helvetica, Arial, sans-
serif

font-size: 2em
```

**Properties** are the first part of the declaration. In this example, our properties are: background-color, font-family, and font-size.

Finally, **values** are the specific styles we want to apply. In this case, our values are: #D9BEE7; Helvetica, sans-serif; and 2em.

Let's now review this by going back to our entire CSS3 example.

```
body
{
background-color: #D9BEE7;
}
p
{
font-family: Helvetica, Arial, sans-
serif;
font-size: 2em;
}
```

The first line tells the computer to look in the HTML5 code for every time it sees the <body> tag. By starting with the word "body" and then using an open curly bracket ( { ) our code first tells the computer to **select** the entire content in our HTML5 file between the <body> start tag and the </body> end tag.

The next few lines **declare** what we want the computer to do with the body text:

```
{
background-color: #D9BEE7;
}
```

In this case, we are telling the computer to display a background color of #D9BEE7. We are calling out the **property** of background-color and assigning it a **value** of #D9BEE7.

**Okay, but what is that jumble of numbers and letters at the end?**

The portion of the code that starts with a hashtag (in this case: #D9BEE7) is what's called the HTML color code (also called a hexadecimal color code or **hex code**, for short).

Hex codes are colors that are used on the web for precise results. For instance, I could theoretically type "background-color: purple" and any one of a gazillion shades of purple might appear. However, if I put in the hex code by instead typing "background-color: #D9BEE7" then a *specific* shade of purple will appear.

In other words, hex codes give computers specific directions on the precise colors and shades you want to appear on the screen.

Hex codes are six-digit hexadecimals (using numbers and letters) and refer to the combination of red, green, and blue (RGB) shading that are present in the color. If you're really curious about the math behind hex codes, you can do calculations to get to the precise color you're seeking. All you really need to know, however, is that you can use a tool such as HTMLcolorcodes.com to select any shade of the rainbow and find out its associated hex color value.

See this article in Smashing Magazine by Ben Gremillion that describes hex codes much better than I ever could: https://www.smashingmagazine.com/2012/10/the-code-side-of-color/.

There are also tons of online resources for selecting hex codes and creating beautiful design palettes. One of my favorites is Adobe Color (https://color.adobe.com/create/color-wheel) , which lets you pick a color—say, a deep shade of red—and then click through tons of options for complementary colors and palettes with that tone.

Canva.com has an excellent article about the various ways websites use hex codes to create beautiful design palettes. See this link if you're interested in reading it: https://www.canva.com/learn/website-color-schemes/.

**Now let's break down the rest.**

Going back to our code, we are left with this:

```
p
{
font-family: Helvetica, Arial, sans-
serif;
font-size: 2em;
}
```

Once again, the p comes before the curly bracket so we know it's the **selector**. It's telling the computer to select all of the text we've included in our HTML5 pages between the tags <p> and </p>.

The final four lines make up our **declaration block**.

First, we **declare** that we want the font-family (the **property** that defines font faces and styles) to be Helvetica font (the **value**). If a browser can't display Helvetica, then we're telling it to use Arial. If the browser also can't display Arial, then we're telling it to choose a sans-serif font to display:

```
{
font-family: Helvetica, Arial, sans-
serif;
```

Note that the order of the fonts (and font styles) you choose matters. The computer will start with the first and if that doesn't work go to the second, and so on. The font-family property can be used generically (e.g., serif or cursive) or more specifically (e.g., Georgia or Times New Roman).

Here is a link to more information about the font-family property, including some examples of some of the more common options: https://developer.mozilla.org/en-US/docs/Web/CSS/font-family.

*Note: If you're new to font design including differences between serif and sans serif fonts, or would simply like a refresher, see this article for more information: https://www.fonts.com/content/learning/fontology/level-1/type-anatomy/serif-vs-sans-for-text-in-print.*

Next, we **declare** that we also want the font-size for all information between the <p> and </p> tags to be displayed in 2em size:

```
font-size: 2em;
}
```

**Wait, what? 2em?**

The value **em** is the commonly accepted standard for calling out font size in CSS3. The number before it is exponential and scalable, depending on how large you want your font to be.

In short, 1em is the standard, normal font size of the screen you're using to view your content—whether on a desktop computer, a laptop, or a mobile device. 2em is twice the size; 2.5em is 2-1/2 times the standard, normal viewing size; 3em is three times the size; and so on. That is, instead of saying you want the size of the font to be 30px (30 pixels) in size—which would appear as 30px in any device—using the em value (such as 1em or 2em) means that the sizing of the font will be relative depending on the size of the device that the audience is using to view the website.

For example, the default font size in web browsers is the equivalent of 16px, so 1em would be the same size as 16px.

The em value can be used in any increments, even going below 1. So, you might use 0.8em if you want the font to be approximately 80% the size of the "normal" viewing font on the screen.

The reason this is important is because of accessibility and **responsive website design**. Responsive website design is flexible website design. It means that the design of a website should respond to the environment and technology that a person is using while accessing the site. You know those websites that look good even on your phone—the ones that adapt based on which device you're using (e.g., laptop, desktop, tablet, phone) and are still accessible and usable? Those are responsive websites, and it means that you don't have to create multiple websites for multiple contexts... that is, if you design it right the first time.

You'll learn more about responsive web design and using em (and other values) for designing accessible, responsive websites in Chapter 6.

To learn more about the em value in CSS3, here is a great article that describes what em is and why it is best used in CSS3 to describe font size: https://www.w3.org/Style/Examples/007/units.en.html.

And here's another great little article that describes the terms related to the CSS3 property of font-size: https://kyleschaeffer.com/css-font-size-em-vs-px-vs-pt-vs-percent.

 *Tip: To see this in action, go back to your main.css file and fiddle with the 2em number. Try changing it to 4em, save the file, and then reload index.html in your web browser. See how much larger the font is? Now, try 1em and see what the "normal" size font looks like on your screen. Try various numbers and increments to see how it affects the size and viewing on your screen.*

## Customizing Your HTML5 and CSS3

Now that you have a sense of what HTML5 and CSS3 can do, it's time to extend the above examples, learn some additional HTML5 tags and CSS3 properties, and create your own files.

*Tip*: Be sure to save your work as you go.

## Step 1: Modifying Your HTML5 Page

- First, make a copy of the files and folder you used in the previous parts of this chapter. There are a few ways to do this; however, this is how I suggest you do it:

- Use Windows Explorer (PC) or Finder (Mac) and navigate to where you've saved your files and folders so far. If you used the previous naming examples, everything should be in a folder called codingproject01.

- Copy that entire folder—which will included your index.html file, css folder, and main.css file—and paste it somewhere else.

- Rename your folder to something new that you'll remember. I recommend something like codingproject02.

- Now, open your new index.html file (located in the codingproject02 folder) in Notepad++ or the text editor of your choice. Remember to keep the name as **index.html**. Your code at this point should still look like this:

```
<!DOCTYPE html>
<html>
  <head>
     <title>My Personal Website</title>
    <link rel="stylesheet"
type="text/css" href="css/main.css" />
  </head>
  <body>
     <p>This is my first basic HTML
page!</p>
  </body>
</html>
```

- Next, you'll change this site to be your first webpage to introduce yourself to the world. To do so, change the title from "My Personal Website" to something more descriptive to you, such as "Dr. Finseth's Website" — which is what I'll call mine in the examples that follow.

  Leave the CSS callout the same for now; we'll modify the CSS next.

- For the body portions, write a short biographical statement and your contact information, using headings and paragraph tags. Specifically:

    o Start with a descriptive heading, by using the tag <h1>. As an example, you might type:

```
<h1>About Me</h1>
```

*Note: <h1> is what is called a Level 1 heading; it will always be the biggest font on the page. The next biggest size is <h2>, then <h3>, and so on. For accessibility reasons, you must always use them in order; that is, h1 will always come before h2, which will always come before h3, etc. You will use your CSS to specifically design the font size and style for each of your headings. We'll do that in the next portion of this project.*

    o Next, write at least one paragraph about yourself, using the **<p>** tag.

    o Then, use the **<h2>** tag to create at least one subheading.

    o After that, write at least one paragraph under that subheading, again using the **<p>** tag.

- o Also put your contact information somewhere on the page, including a **hyperlink** to your email address. The code for hyperlinking to an email address is **<a href="mailto:emailaddress">**. For example:

```
<a
href="mailto:carly@finsethconsulting.co
m">carly@finsethconsulting.com</a>
```

  Whatever you put between the <a> tags is what users will see on the screen. In the above example they'll simply see hyperlinked text that looks like this: carly@finsethconsulting.com.

- Next, **add at least one more hyperlink** to your code. Just like the email link, it will start with <a href. However, instead of mailto: you will use http://. Here is an example:

```
<a
href="http://www.mcfarlandbooks.com"
target="_blank">McFarland Books</a>
```

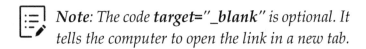 *Note: The code **target="_blank"** is optional. It tells the computer to open the link in a new tab.*

- Finally, practice and include a few more common HTML5 tags somewhere in your page. These include:

  - **<em>** for italic text;

  - **<strong>** for bold text; and

  - **<hr />** for a horizontal rule.

    Both **<em>** and **<strong>** are used inside of the <p> tags, when you want to emphasize certain words and phrases. For the purposes of this project, try practicing them at least once. They're a few of the only ways that you add styling elements to your text outside of CSS.

    **<hr />** is a unique tag that encompasses the start tag and end tag together in one. This is because you don't need to add extra content inside of a horizontal rule; all you want it to do is add a line.

## Example

As an example of putting all of the above together, here is what my example file would look like:

```
<!DOCTYPE html>
<html>
<head>
<title>Dr. Finseth's Website</title>
<link rel="stylesheet" type="text/css"
href="css/main.css" />
</head>
<body>
<h1>About Me</h1>
<p>I'm a nationally-recognized author,
educator, researcher, and consultant. In my
academic consulting practice, I bring a mix
of professional and academic expertise to
provide custom solutions for my clients.</p>
<p>Previously, I was the Senior Vice
President of Education at Northwest Lineman
College (NLC), a Quanta Services Company. In
this role, I led and developed educational
standards of excellence for the power
delivery, gas, and telecommunications
industries. I was responsible for curriculum
development, corporate learning and
development, and business-to-consumer
educational programs.</p>
<p>Before my executive career, I was an
award-winning tenure-track professor. I also
have more than 15 years of additional
industry experience, including project
management, women-focused leadership and
entrepreneurship, and editing and
publications management. I have been a
freelance writer, editor, and designer for
```

```
20 years and counting. My first book,
<em>Teach Like a Gamer: Adapting the
Instructional Design of Digital Role-Playing
Games</em>, was published in 2018 by <a
href="http://www.mcfarlandbooks.com''
target="_blank">McFarland Books</a>.</p>
<hr />
<h2>Contact Me</h2>
<p>To learn more or to inquire about my
consulting services, feel free to contact me
via phone at (208) 877-3287 or via email at
<a
href="mailto:carly@finsethconsulting.com">ca
rly@finsethconsulting.com</a>.</p>
</body>
</html>
```

- **Don't forget to save your file**. Remember it must be called **index.html**.

- As a final step, open the file in your browser and test your code. For instance, when I open my file, it looks like this:

**About Me**

I'm a nationally-recognized author, educator, researcher, and consultant. In my academic consulting practice, I bring a mix of professional and academic expertise to provide custom solutions for my clients.

Previously, I was the Senior Vice President of Education at Northwest Lineman College (NLC), a Quanta Services Company. In this role, I led and developed educational standards of excellence for the power delivery, gas, and telecommunications industries. I was responsible for curriculum development, corporate learning and development, and business-to-consumer educational programs.

Before my executive career, I was an award-winning tenure-track professor. I also have more than 15 years of additional industry experience, including project management, women-focused leadership and entrepreneurship, and editing and publications management. I have been a freelance writer, editor, and designer for 20 years and counting. My first book, *Teach Like a Gamer: Adapting the Instructional Design of Digital Role-Playing Games*, was published in 2018 by McFarland Books.

**Contact Me**

To learn more or to inquire about my consulting services, feel free to contact me via phone at (208) 877-3287 or via email at carly@finsethconsulting.com.

## Step 2: Modifying Your CSS File

Now that you have your HTML content ready, it's time to style it using CSS.

- First, open your new **main.css** file. (If you've used the above examples, it will be located in the codingproject02 folder, inside a folder called css.) Remember to keep the name as main.css. Your code at this point should still look like this:

```
body
{
background-color: #D9BEE7;
}
p
{
font-family: Helvetica, Arial, sans-
serif;
font-size: 2em;
}
```

- Now it's time to change the values and add a few more. First, change the background color. Go to HTMLColorCodes.com (or another resource of your choice) and find a color you like; then change the #D9BEE7 value to your new color choice.

- Next, change your font choice(s). Here are a few common ones to consider:

```
font-family: Times, Times New Roman,
Georgia, serif;
font-family: Palatino Linotype, Book
Antiqua, Palatino, serif;
font-family: Verdana, Arial, Helvetica,
sans-serif;
font-family: Impact, Charcoal, sans-
serif;
font-family: Tahoma, Geneva, sans-
serif;
font-family: Trebuchet MS, Helvetica,
sans-serif;
font-family: Lucida Console, Courier,
monospace;
font-family: Courier New, Courier,
monospace;
font-family: cursive;
font-family: fantasy;
```

*Note: I suggest experimenting with these font family choices by changing your CSS and reloading your index.html file in your browser, so you can choose the look that you like best.*

Feel free to experiment with a variety of font combinations; however, there are two things to consider:

  o Choose one type of style (e.g., serif, sans-serif, or monospace).

o Start with what is called a "**web safe font**"; those are fonts that are universally considered to be loadable on everyone's computer and therefore usable on the web.

Here is a list of 15 web safe fonts that I suggest you start with: https://websitesetup.org/web-safe-fonts-html-css/. As you're learning I suggest you use at least one web safe font. After that, you can experiment with any open font you like, such as a Google font (https://fonts.google.com/).

As an example, let's say you love the Google font Open Sans. You might type this into your CSS:

```
font-family: Open Sans, Helvetica,
Arial, sans-serif;
```

This tells the computer that, if available, it should display the content in Open Sans. If the user doesn't have that, then please load it in Helvetica. If they still don't have that, then load the content in Arial. Almost everyone should have Arial on their computers. But, just in case they don't, the "sans-serif" callout at the end will find *something* on the user's device that will match that style as closely as possible.

- Now that you've chosen a font-family, you should also practice changing the size of the font. So, instead of 2em pick something bigger or smaller than that.

- Test. Again, I'd suggest opening your index.html file in your browser, modifying your CSS, and then reloading the index.html file (by pressing F5 on your keyboard) to see what it looks like.

- Next, add some CSS lines that tell the computer how to style your <h1> and <h2> headings. To do so, add these lines to the bottom of your main.css file:

```
h1, h2 {
  color: #05082E;
  font-family: Times, Times New Roman,
Georgia, serif;
}
h1 {
  font-size: 2em;
}

h2 {
  font-size: 1.75em;
}
```

These lines will tell the computer how to style the headings of your HTML. Feel free to modify the color

(I simply used #05082E for my example), the font-family, and the font-sizes to suit your style.

- Then, you'll add another few lines of code to tell the CSS how to style the horizontal rule <hr /> you entered into the page. Type in the following code at the end of your **main.css** file:

```
hr {
  border-top: dotted 2px #8c8b8b;
  border-bottom: solid 2px #ECECEC;
}
```

This tells the code to put a border on the bottom of the horizontal rule. The **border-top** code tells the computer to put a border at the top of the line. I've told it to be a dotted line, 2px tall, in the color #8c8b8b. The **border-bottom** code adds a solid line that is 2px tall, and is in the color #ECECEC.

Again, feel free to modify the color and size/style of your horizontal rule.

For style, you can choose from: dotted, solid, dashed, or double.

Feel free to change the sizes of the lines and the hex code(s) of the colors.

- Finally, add a few lines of CSS to tell the page how you want to style your hyperlinks. Copy and paste the following code at the end of your CSS:

```
a {
  outline: none;
  text-decoration: none;
  font-weight: bold;
}
a:link {
  color: #FF5733;
  border-bottom: 1px solid;
}
a:visited {
  color: #9B59B6;
}
a:hover {
  color: #3498DB;
}
```

You'll notice there are a few different things this code is doing. At first, the "a" code is simply defining how you want all links to look. In this case, we don't want any outlines (such as a box around the text); and we don't want any "decoration" (e.g., wavy, dashed, or dotted text). For the link itself, there are three different behaviors we're defining:

- o **a:link**: this defines the properties of the link itself, before a user has clicked on it. Here, I've defined a color, as well as a 1px size solid underline.

o **a:visited**: this defines the properties of the link after a user has clicked on it. Here, I've said I want it to be a different color, with no underline.

o **a: hover**: this defines the properties of the link when a user hovers over it. Here, I've defined a new color that will show when a user hovers their mouse over the link.

Once again, fiddle with these properties and come up with your own color and style combinations to suit the rest of your page.

• **Don't forget to save your file!** As a reminder, it should be saved as **main.css**.

**Example CSS Modification**

Using the above examples, my new CSS code looks like this:

```
body
{
background-color: #DAF7A6;
}
p
{
font-family: Palatino Linotype, Book
Antiqua, Palatino, serif;
font-size: 1.2em;
}
 h1, h2 {
 color: #05082E;
 font-family: Verdana, Arial,
```

```
 Helvetica, sans-serif;
 }
 h1 {
  font-size: 2em;
 }

 h2 {
  font-size: 1.75em;
 }
   hr {
  border-top: dotted 2px #8c8b8b;
  border-bottom: solid 2px #ECECEC;
 }
 a {
  outline: none;
  text-decoration: none;
  font-weight: bold;
 }
 a:link {
  color: #FF5733;
  border-bottom: 1px solid;
 }
 a:visited {
  color: #9B59B6;
 }
 a:hover {
  color: #3498DB;
 }
```

As a result, once I refresh my index.html file in my browser, it now looks like this:

**About Me**

I'm a nationally-recognized author, educator, researcher, and consultant. In my academic consulting practice, I bring a mix of professional and academic expertise to provide custom solutions for my clients.

Previously, I was the Senior Vice President of Education at Northwest Lineman College (NLC), a Quanta Services Company. In this role, I led and developed educational standards of excellence for the power delivery, gas, and telecommunications industries. I was responsible for curriculum development, corporate learning and development, and business-to-consumer educational programs.

Before my executive career, I was an award-winning tenure-track professor. I also have more than 15 years of additional industry experience, including project management, women-focused leadership and entrepreneurship, and editing and publications management. I have been a freelance writer, editor, and designer for 20 years and counting. My first book, *Teach Like a Game: Adapting the Instructional Design of Digital Role-Playing Games*, was published in 2018 by McFarland Books.

**Contact Me**

To learn more or to inquire about my consulting services, feel free to contact me via phone at (208) 877-3287 or via email at carly@finsettconsulting.com.

Note we aren't worried so much about aesthetics at this point, but rather are looking to master how HTML and CSS work together, as well as learning basic HTML tags and adding various styles through CSS. (With that said, yours will likely look prettier than mine.)

The key here is you've made meaningful changes using HTML5 and CSS3. Have you learned to change fonts? Colors? Styles? That's the key for this chapter.

## Ta-Da!

You've now created your first HTML5 and CSS3 documents and have put them all together to create your very first webpage.

In the next chapter, you'll build on these new skills to learn some intermediate skills in both languages, including adding images, videos, tables, borders, and more. You'll also build a multiple page website of your very own.

# CHAPTER 6
# MASTERING INTERMEDIATE SKILLS
# IN HTML5 AND CSS3

## What You'll Learn

- How to build a website with multiple pages, using HTML5 and CSS3.
- How to write code that is readable for others.
- How to add images, videos, documents, and menus to your website.
- How to create tables, lists, spacing, borders, and other elements of layout to your pages.
- How to ensure your content is accessible for all viewers.

## What You'll Create

By the end of this chapter, you will have coded a multiple-page website using HTML5 and CSS3.

## Required Tools and Supplies

You will need access to a good text editor, such as Notepad++, as well as access to at least one web browser. See Chapter 1 for download information.

You will also need some various online reference guides, which I'll link to throughout this chapter.

## Optional Tools and Supplies

Although it's not required, you may want to have an additional book or handbook at your side, depending on your learning style. As mentioned in Chapter 5, here are a few of my favorites:

*HTML and CSS* by **Jon Duckett**

*Build Your Own Website: A Comic Guide to HTML, CSS, and WordPress* by **Nate Cooper with Art by Kim Gee**

## Coding is Writing

The ultimate goal of this chapter will be for you to create a multiple page website on your own. First, though, you'll need to learn some more of the beginning to intermediate coding skills in HTML5 and CSS3 to make it happen.

To start, it's important you understand that coding is just another form of writing. It needs to be readable, usable, and accessible to your users—both on the front-end (which is the website viewers see) and the back-end (which is the code you see on the development side).

> **Note**: *Coding Horror wrote a great article on this called "Coding: It's Just Writing." Here's the link if you're interested in reading more: https://blog.codinghorror .com/coding-its-just-writing/ .*

There are two ways you can make your code more readable and usable: using a text editor and making comment tags.

Using a text editor can add some color and formatting to help you (and other potential readers) follow along with your code. This includes using the tab key and spacing wisely, too.

Although this is personal preference, I believe that using tabs and coloring in Notepad++ (and other advanced text editors) helps you become a better coder. It makes your code cleaner and easier to read, as well as makes it overall easier to catch any potential mistakes. Plus, you may notice a few other things of note, such as there are numbers along the left-hand side of the Notepad++ interface. Those call out the numeric lines of code so you can easily reference them in your code or elsewhere.

The second way to make your code more readable and usable is to use **comment tags** to leave notes for yourself. Comment tags look like this:

```
<!-- -->
```

We'll talk more about how and why to use comment tags in the next section.

## Using Comment Tags to Organize Your Writing

In HTML, everything between the <!-- and the --> are comments that only you or anyone else reading the back-end of your code can read. It does not show up on the front-end of your website. This means it isn't published online or visible to regular viewers, but can serve as important notes and milestones for yourself and other coders.

This is enormously helpful for annotating your code so that others can understand it. For example, it's common to write things like:

```
<!-- Table starts here -->
```

This is so you can keep track of where a table starts in your document, and also where others can find it.

In other words, the comment tag functions quite similarly to using headings in technical documents—it helps organize your thoughts and helps you and others easily track your way in a document.

To the computer, the comment tag indicates it should ignore that text—so really you can write whatever you want in within the comment tags that will help you organize your thoughts and your code.

Comment tags are also good ways to test and debug your code if something goes wrong. For instance, maybe your page is rendering incorrectly but you can't figure out why. You can use the comment tags to turn some of your code on and off, to see which part(s) may be triggering the error.

```
<!-- Whatever I write within these tags
the computer will ignore. This is a good
opportunity to make notes for myself.
-->
```

### Adding Comment Tags in CSS3

You can also add comment tags in CSS3. They look like this: /* */. Everything between the /* and the */ is ignored by the computer and is used solely for your own information. For instance:

```
/* Here is some code I might add so I
can remember to come back to this
later, or maybe I want to use it as a
heading */
```

## The Line Break

In Chapter 5 we discussed the horizontal rule, or <hr />. Another tag to keep handy in your toolkit is line break, or **<br />**. Just like <hr />, <br /> is a start and an end tag all on its own. To add an extra line between content, simply type:

```
<br />
```

## Effectively Using Blockquotes

Another useful HTML5 tag to know is the <blockquote> tag. Technically, in HTML5 you would use the <blockquote> tag when setting off a quote from another source, like this:

```
<blockquote>Here's a quote from another
source.</blockquote>
```

However, you can also use it in any context as a design element, if you'd like to have the tabbed-in look, such as:

```
<blockquote> Lorem ipsum dolor sit
amet, consectetur adipiscing elit.
Phasellus facilisis ornare imperdiet.
Donec dignissim magna ac lorem
fermentum, eget ullamcorper magna
facilisis. Donec id fringilla augue.
Nulla imperdiet nibh risus, ullamcorper
fringilla urna auctor sed. In tristique
mattis leo, at malesuada mi auctor ut.
Proin eget pretium felis, vel accumsan
tortor. Sed at diam semper, porttitor
turpis in, tempor lorem. Vestibulum ac
rutrum elit.</blockquote>
```

To do so, simply put the content you'd like to have indented between the <blockquote> and </blockquote> tags.

## Creating Lists

Every self-respecting technical communicator understands the importance of a good list. That's why you'll also need to know how to code one in HTML.

### How to Make a Bulleted List

For a bulleted list, you start with **<ul>**. Then, each list item starts with **<li>** and ends with </li>. End the entire list with the closing tag of </ul>. Therefore, a bulleted list may look like this:

```
<ul>
<li>Here's a list item.</li>
<li>Here's another list item.</li>
<li>And here's another list item.</li>
</ul>
```

The result would look like this in a web browser:

- Here's a list item.
- Here's another list item.
- And here's another list item.

### How to Make a Numbered List

To make it into a numbered list instead of a bulleted list, you'd simply change the <ul> to an **<ol>**, like this:

```
<ol>
<li>Here's a list item.</li>
<li>Here's another list item.</li>
<li>And here's another list item.</li>
</ol>
```

The result then leaves you with this in a web browser:

1. Here's a list item.
2. Here's another list item.
3. And here's another list item.

## Designing a Table

Most technical communicators I know value a good table for when you need to organize data or information.

To do so, you use the <table> tag, along with its friends <thead> and <th> (table headings) for headings, and <tbody> (table body content), <tr> (table row), and <td> (table cell) for the major content of your table.

A typical table might look something like this:

```
<table>
 <thead>
   <th>Name</th>
   <th>Personality Type</th>
   <th>Personality Traits</th>
 </thead>
 <tbody>
   <tr>
     <td>Sheri Drayton</td>
     <td>ESFJ</td>
     <td>Outgoing, social, open</td>
```

```
    </tr>
    <tr>
      <td>Pilar Chaudry</td>
      <td>EITP</td>
      <td>Insensitive, assertive,
attention seeking</td>
    </tr>
    <tr>
      <td>Skye Barber</td>
      <td>EIFP</td>
      <td>Disorganized, empathetic,
idealistic</td>
    </tr>
    <tr>
      <td>Marvin Campbell</td>
      <td>ESTJ</td>
      <td>Controlling, practical,
traditional</td>
    </tr>
  </tbody>
</table>
```

The **<thead>** entries define the table's top labels. <tr> starts a new row. And **<td>** is the content in the table's cell itself. In a web browser, the above would look like this:

| Name | Personality Type | Personality Traits |
|------|------------------|--------------------|
| Sheri Drayton | ESFJ | Outgoing, social, open |
| Pilar Chaudry | EITP | Insensitive, assertive, attention seeking |
| Skye Barber | EIFP | Disorganized, empathetic, idealistic |
| Marvin Campbell | ESTJ | Controlling, practical, traditional |

You can probably tell the table in its current form isn't very pretty, and the alignment seems off. We can fix that using CSS3.

*:≡/* **Note:** *When HTML was first created, tables were used to control the placement of text and elements on the screen. It's no longer used in that way. Now, tables are used in HTML5 how we think of them in technical communication: as means for displaying and organizing data in an easy-to-read format. Therefore, don't ever use tables in HTML5 simply to align or move images or text; instead, use CSS3 for that. (You'll learn more on how to do that in the next section.)*

## Formatting Tables Using CSS3

It perhaps goes without saying—but I'll say it here anyway—that just like you learned in the previous chapter, you will have a main.css file to go with your index.html (and other .html) files.

In your main.css file, you will want to add code that tells the computer how to style your tables (just like you'll tell it how to style everything else—such as body text, paragraphs, and headers).

To format tables in CSS, you use a series of commands that can tell the computer how to space and organize your data.

For instance, you might add CSS code to main.css that looks like this:

```
table {
 table-layout: fixed;
 width: 100%;
 border-collapse: collapse;
 border: 3px solid #000;
}
thead th:nth-child(1) {
 width: 15%;
}

thead th:nth-child(2) {
 width: 10%;
}

thead th:nth-child(3) {
 width: 25%;
}

th {
 text-align: left;
 padding: 20px;
 border-collapse: collapse;
 border: 3px solid #000;
 background-color: #ECECEC;
}

td {
 text-align: left;
 padding: 20px;
 border-collapse: collapse;
 border: 1px solid #000;
}
```

You'll notice some different callouts here, which tell the computer how to format and style the table.

First, we've used **table-layout: fixed**, which tells the computer to fix the widths of the columns based on percentages (or pixels) that you will define later. The other option is **table-layout: auto** (wherein the widths are determined automatically by the computer). I'd recommend using table-layout: fixed for now, which gives you a bit more control as a developer.

The **border-collapse** property defines whether you want the tables borders to be separated. Your options are:

- **border-collapse: collapse**—which means the cells will share borders; or

- **border-collapse: separate**—which means there will be separate borders around each cell.

Under that, we've defined the border size (if you want a border) and color, using a hex code. Here I'm saying to use a 3px wide line as the border, in color #000000 (black).

*Note: If you're using a hex code with repeating numbers, you can also write it using just the first three. So, #000000 is also #000, #ffffff is also #fff, and so on. If you only use three digits the computer will automatically fill in the last three by repeating the first three again.*

Next, we've specified exact **percentages** of how we want the table to display on a screen. By using percentages—such as 20%, 15%, and 35%—we've made the design responsive, meaning it will expand or contract based on the size of screen the viewer is using (e.g., 35% means that the table column will expand or contract to be 35% of the screen size—whether on a desktop monitor, a laptop screen, a tablet, or a phone).

By defining **nth-child**, we are specifying the exact columns—in order, from left to right—that we want to size. For instance, nth-child(1) is the first column, nth-child(2) is the second column, and nth-child(3) is the third column.

Under **th**, we have defined a few things: **text-align**, which tells it which alignment you'd like for the text (choices are left, right, or center).

We've also defined the **padding** to be 20px. This means that the computer will add 20px of space all around the contents in both the headers and cells, so that the text doesn't run into the walls of the table border or into text from other cells. You can define this however you like—from no padding at all (0px or leaving it out) to as high as you like. Once again, we define a **border**; and this time we've added a **background color** for the header cells.

Finally, under **td**, we have repeated some of those same attributes but have changed a few things, such as making the border a bit smaller (1px instead of 3px).

Here's what the result now looks like in a browser:

| Name | Personality Type | Personality Traits |
| --- | --- | --- |
| Sheri Drayton | ESFJ | Outgoing, social, open |
| Pilar Chaudry | INTP | Inventive, assertive, attention seeking |
| Skye Barber | ENFP | Disorganized, empathetic, idealistic |
| Martin Campbell | ESTJ | Controlling, practical, traditional |

As with other HTML5 and CSS3 code, I suggest you take some time to experiment with various tags, elements, and styles.

Here is a resource with additional information on styling

tables in HTML5 and CSS3: https://developer.mozilla. org/en-US/docs/Learn/CSS/Building blocks/Styling tables.

## Linking to Other Pages

Previously you learned how to create a link to an email address or website. As a refresher, an email link looks like this:

```
<a
href="mailto:carly@finsethconsulting.co
m">carly@finsethconsulting.com</a>
```

And a website link looks like this:

```
<a href="http://finsethconsulting.com"
target="_blank">finsethconsulting.com</
a>
```

In the above example, target="_blank" will make the link open in a new tab. You can leave it out if you don't want the link to open in a new tab.

What if you want the link to go to another page on your site? The first option is that you could put in the whole URL, if you want:

```
<a
href="http://websiteexample.com/about">
About Page</a>
```

But that is a clunky solution and requires your computer to do more work. A better option is to just link to the page itself in relation to where it's located on your site's hierarchy.

For example, let's say that you have the following .html files as part of your website, and they're all saved in the same folder:

- index.html

- about.html

- contact.html

You want to add a link on your index.html page that will directly go to your contact.html page. Here's how you'd do it:

```
<a href="about.html">About Page</a>
```

Now, that only works if index.html and about.html are organized in the same folder. But what if you have the about.html page inside a folder called "pages"? The link would then look like this:

```
<a href="pages/about.html">About Page</a>
```

In other words, adding links is all about the **relative position** of where the link is in relation to your site.

## File Paths and Linking to Documents like PDFs

This same technique for linking works with any elements of your site—whether an .html page, an image, a media file, or a document.

Imagine that you have the following structure set up on your site, with folders called "css," "documents," and "images." You want to add to your index.html page a link to a document in your "documents" folder called "resume.pdf." You would have to type in the structure of where "resume.pdf" is in relation to the index.html file, like this:

```
<a href="documents/resume.pdf">Click here to view my resume in PDF format.</a>
```

Okay, but what if the opposite is true? Well, to move backward in a site's folder hierarchy, you use two dots, like this:

```
<a href="../resume.pdf">This link would go back one folder to find a file called resume.pdf.</a>
```

This is why it's so crucial you set up a smart workspace and know where you've saved and organized your files.

Linking to content—such as other .html pages, images, media content, and documents on your site can easily be done if you know the file path.

This site has more information on file paths, if you're curious: https://developer.mozilla.org/en-US/docs/ Learn/HTML/Introduction_to_HTML/Creating_hyperlinks# a_quick_primer_on_urls_and_paths.

## Adding Images

One of the fundamental skills in building websites is knowing how to insert images and other media into your pages. To do so, use the **<img src>** tag, which stands for image, source. That is, you're telling the computer you want to insert an image and then you'll tell it where to source (or get) that image. To do so, you'll use file paths to tell it where to get your images.

As an example, this code is saying to look inside the media folder and find the image of a tree that I've named tree.jpg:

```
<img src="media/tree.jpg">
```

-☀- *Tip*: *Although many types of images are possible to use on websites, I recommend always using .jpg or .png files, which render best and fastest online. I also recommend always storing your images in your media folder, so you know where to find and easily access them.*

⚠ ***Important Note***: *Don't ever link to images from other websites. Aside from potential copyright violations, that's an unethical process called "hotlinking." Instead, always host images on your own website and link to them from there.*

## Ensuring Your Content Is Accessible

As a web developer, I believe you have a responsibility for ensuring your content is viewable by all users. This means creating a website with content that is readable by people from all backgrounds and means of accessibility, including those who are visually or hearing impaired or who may use screen readers or other accessibility software to navigate your site. To do so, there are some elements you'll want to always ensure you include in your code.

### Making Images Accessible

Equally important to providing the right file path for your image is to provide descriptive alternate text that describes for screen readers (or in other instances, when the image won't load) what the image is. To do so, you use an attribute called the **alt tag**. The alt tag gets nested inside the <img src> tag, like this:

```
<img src="media/tree.jpg" alt="An
image of a large oak tree in the fall,
with broad orange leaves">
```

It's important you make your alt tag as descriptive as possible so your images are accessible to others.

For more information and examples on inserting images into your pages and using alt text, see this link: https://developer.mozilla.org/en-US/docs/Learn/HTML/ Multimedia and embedding/Images in HTML.

## Making Videos Accessible

It's also important if you host videos on your website to ensure they are accessible to your users. This involves two things:

- Making sure your video has captions; and

- Hosting a transcript of the video somewhere on your site. This can be in HTML format (preferred) or in a Word .doc that is downloadable.

## Making PDFs Accessible

Finally, if you include PDFs on your site, it's also crucial to provide a version that is accessible for your users.

A common misconception is you can use tags in your PDF file or use tools—such as what's available in Adobe Acrobat Pro—to make the PDF itself accessible. This works to a certain extent—but most screen readers still aren't advanced enough to read the content.

Blind users have told me personally that the only way to make your PDFs accessible is to convert them to Word format. That is, PDFs aren't accessible, regardless of what some companies claim.

It's always good practice to ensure accessibility of your web content by providing either an HTML transcript or Word document in addition to, or in place of, a PDF.

> *Tip:* To see this in action, try it out. Download a free screen reader and try "reading" an "accessible PDF" and hear what happens. Popular screen readers include NVDA, Jaws, Cobra, Dolphin Screen Reader, Serotek, BRLTTY, ORCA, Apple VoiceOver (iOS), and ChromeVox (Google Chromebook).

### Additional Usability and Accessibility Considerations

There is enough information about making sites usable and accessible that I could make an entire book about it. In fact, there are many articles and stand-alone books that already exist on the topic.

If you'd like to learn more, I suggest you read this short blog post by Cody Ray Miller entitled "Website Navigation: 4 Tips for Maximum Usability": https://www.crazyegg.com/blog/website-navigation/.

One of my favorite stand-alone books on the subject is *A Web for Everyone: Designing Accessible User Experiences* **by Sarah Horton and Whitney Quesenbery**.

## Adding Structure and Layout to Your Pages

In HTML5, there are several tags that provide structure and organization to your content pages. These include:

- **<header>**: A header is where you put the title and other heading information about what's on your page.

- **<main>**: This is where all of the main content of your site exists. It usually comes right below the <header> of your file.

- **<section>**: This defines a chunk of content or information that all belongs together. It's common to put a heading first (e.g., <h1> or <h2>) and then use <section> for the information that belongs under that header.

- **<article>**: This is a bit more nebulous, but is used for content that could be syndicated or reused somewhere else. This might be useful if you've written something that you imagine being repurposed somewhere else, such as published on another site or in another context, such as a copyright notice, an article, or a blog post. Unlike <section>, which can be used to organize your content in any way you like, think of <article> as content that would stand alone contextually, even if posted somewhere else besides your website.

- **<aside>**: Although only sparingly used in my experience, this tag can identify information that's a bit of a side note or regression from the rest of the content. That is, something that's tangentially related to the other content. Maybe you'd use this for a footnote, tip, or side note.

- **<nav>**: Short for navigation, the <nav> tag is used to set off things like a Table of Contents or a menu. Typically, a bulleted list would go inside the tags. It's used for helping users navigate your site and its content.

*Note: There are many ways you can style <nav> tag to make horizontal or vertical menus on your site. Rather than go into all of that here, I suggest reading this short tutorial, which includes practice areas to see what you can do with HTML5 and CSS3 to make great-looking menus on your site.*

- **<footer>**: This is often used for a bottom navigation (menu) area or a copyright notice—anything that would go at the very bottom of the page.

- **<div>**: The <div> tag used to be used for all structure and layout (and it still works in that way); however, HTML5 dictates that we now only use <div> if it's to structure or organize an element of your page that otherwise wouldn't need a heading tag (e.g., <h1>, <h2>, etc.), in which case you would use <section> instead, or wouldn't be content that was syndicated elsewhere, in which case you would use <article> instead. In other words, only use this if one of the other above tags doesn't apply.

*Note: Many people use <div> in place of almost all of the other tags introduced in this section—and you'll see this a lot in older websites, as there hasn't yet been a reason for web developers to go back and retroactively change their code. Therefore, if you see <div> in code that you're reading or modifying, know that it still works, but elements such as <section> and <article> have since been introduced to make code easier to organize and read.*

Each of the above tags would be directly linked to a sister CSS3 entry that would define the unique styling, layout, borders, and so on for that portion of the page.

## Example of a Structured HTML Page

Let's look at some code that includes all of the above:

```
<article>
 <header>
   <h1>A Descriptive Heading for My
Website Content</h1>
 </header>
<main>
 <div class="menu">
 <p>Here's a menu:</p>
 <nav class="menu">
    <ul>
     <li><a
href="#intro">Introduction</a>
     <li><a href="#context">Context</a>
     <li><a href="#footer">Footer</a>
    </ul>
 </nav>
 </div>
 <section id="intro"
class="introduction">
   <h2>Introduction to My Terrific
Website</h2>
     <p>I'd put some really fascinating
content here.</p>
     <p>Ooh, and then I'd
<em>really</em> say something cool and
interesting here, too.</p>
     <p>In this part I'd also say
something that's riveting for my
```

```
audience.</p>
    <article id="context">
    <h2>An Excellent Article</h2>
        <p>This part gives some really
excellent detail, in a standalone
context, that maybe could be published
somewhere else.</p>
        <aside>
        <h3>An Awesome Side Note</h3>
            <p>Here's something
tangentially related to the article.
It's somewhat interesting, but a bit of
a tangent.</p>
        </aside>
    </article>
  </section>
</main>
  <footer id="footer">
    <p>Posted by Carly Finseth</p>
  </footer>
</article>
```

If you're paying attention—and I hope you are—you'll notice I've used **id** and **class** tags here and there within my tags. These can be called out individually in the CSS, to style things in various ways.

In CSS, a class selector starts off with a period (e.g., .introduction) and an ID selector starts off with a hashtag (e.g., #intro). So, our CSS might look like this:

```
#intro {
    background-color: #ffffff;
    padding: 10px;
}

.introduction {
    color: #ececec;
    font-weight: bold;
}
```

ID selectors (e.g., where I've put an id tag, such as: <footer id="footer">) can also be used for menus to navigate to certain parts of an HTML page. By giving the <footer> tag an ID selector, as in: <footer id="footer">, it means that in my upper menu navigation, I can callout <a href="#footer"> and the computer knows that if the user clicks on that link, it should take them to the part of my HTML page where I've used that ID.

If you use an ID selector, know it must perfectly match wherever you code it, so be on the lookout for potential typos. However, if done well, they can make for really slick navigational tools for your readers to quickly and easily navigate your website. In other words, they're almost like a Table of Contents to quickly let users click around to where they need to go.

## To Learn More

To learn more about any of the above intermediate HTML5 or CSS3 tags, elements, or properties, I suggest using the MDN Web Docs page at https://developer.mozilla.org/en-US/. There, you can search for just about any attribute, tag, element, and so on, and find explanations and examples that may help clarify some of the above concepts for you. It's also a great resource to have on hand so you don't have to memorize everything.

# Coding Your Multi-Page Website

Whew! That was a lot, right? Well, if you understand the above, then you're well on your way to an intermediate-level understanding of HTML5 and CSS3. The next step is for you to practice those skills by coding some of your own pages.

For this chapter's exercise, you will code a website with a minimum of five .html pages and one .css page that interact and link with one another and use a combination of all of the tags and skills you've learned in the previous parts of this chapter.

## Step 1: Choose What to Build

The first step will be to decide what, exactly, your project will be. That is, what type of website will you build, who will be your target audience, and what will be your ultimate purpose for creating it?

Here are a few options to consider:

- A website to showcase a professional portfolio.

- A personal website to feature you and your achievements, resume, and so on.

- A site that showcases something cool you've created, such as a step-by-step tutorial.

- A website for a real or fictional product or service you'd like to offer.

Although what you create is up to you, for now there's only one rule: **The website you choose to build shouldn't require any interactive components, such as commenting.** That's because to add features where users can interact with your content (e.g., a blog), it requires additional coding beyond HTML. (Typically, such features are done using a database and Javascript.)

We don't have time to cover that right now. (And honestly, it's best for you to focus on the basics right now, anyway.) However, if you have access to a web server, a database, and your own resources for learning how to code interactive web content, you're welcome to try.

## Step 2: Create Your Workspace

Just like you've already learned, you'll want to first create your workspace.

Before you get started, open Windows Explorer (for PC users) or Finder (for Mac users) and create the following folder hierarchy:

**Primary project folder**: This can be named anything you like, so long as it only uses lowercase letters, numbers, underscores, or hyphens. Make it as short and as descriptive as possible; for instance: codingproject03. This folder is where you will keep all of your .html files for your project.

Inside your primary project folder, create three additional folders:

- **css**
- **documents**
- **media**

*Note: They should be named this exactly, using lowercase letters. These folders are where you will house your .css files, your documents (such as PDFs or Word .docs), and your multimedia content (such as images and videos), respectively.*

## Step 3: Write and Organize Your Content

Thinking through the appropriate rhetorical situation for your site, you should write and organize your content in such a way that demonstrates at least an intermediate understanding of HTML5 and CSS3.

Try to ensure your writing is clean, organized, and easy to follow. This will mean using tabbing and spacing effectively in your code itself—such as indenting various tags for readability.

It will also mean including comments, so other users can read your code.

I emphasize all of this as a way of building good habits from the start. If you learn to code in a way that is easier to read and correct, it will absolutely help you in the long run.

## What to Include in Your Website

For maximum learning impact, at a *minimum* I suggest you include the following in your website:

- A minimum of five separate **.html** files, including index.html and at least four other .html files.
  - As an example, if you create a portfolio website, you might have index.html as your home page with your introduction and so on, and then additional pages for each deliverable you'd like to introduce and feature. You might also then include an about.html page to tell the viewers a bit about you and your background.

- One **.css** file entitled main.css.

- A **menu**, horizontal or vertical, that is present on every page, that viewers can use to navigate your content.

 *Note: This menu should link all five of your .html pages together, to aid in navigation.*

*Tip: Use <nav> and, if you didn't read it earlier in this book, see this tutorial on how to style various menus, etc.:* https://www.w3schools.com/css/css_navbar.asp.

- At least one image; use **<img src>** and be sure to include a descriptive alt tag so the content is accessible.

- At least three **comment tags** used somewhere in your HTML; and at least three comment tags used in somewhere in your CSS.

- Use at least three of the following additional new skills you learned in this book so far:

  - **<hr />**: horizontal rule

  - **<br />**: line break

  - **<blockquote>**: indented content

  - **<ul>** or **<ol>**: bulleted or numbered list

  - **<table>**: table

  - **<a href>**: link to other pages and/or content

  - **Tags for structure and organization**: <header>, <main>, <section>, <article>, <aside>, <nav>, <footer>, and/or <div>

## Step 4: Test Your Code

Perhaps this goes without saying, but don't forget to save all your work as you go, and also test it in your web browser.

I suggest when you complete a step or section of code that you open files in your browser and make sure it all works before moving on to the next step. This will also help you backtrack, if needed, if any code breaks or has errors.

# Yippee!

If you have completed all of the above, tested your work, and it looks and functions as you'd expect it to: nicely done! You have now demonstrated you understand how to read, write, and modify HTML5 and CSS3 at least an intermediate level.

In the next chapter, you'll learn about HTML templates and how to modify more complex code using advanced techniques.

# CHAPTER 7
# CREATING A CUSTOM WEBSITE
# WITH HTML5 AND CSS3

## What You'll Learn

- How to read and modify complex HTML5 and CSS3.
- How to modify existing templates and add your own custom code to create a new website.
- How to leverage free and open content to make yours truly shine.

## What You'll Create

By the end of this level, you will have created a website from a template, using advanced HTML5 and CSS3.

## Required Tools and Supplies

You will need access to a good text editor, such as Notepad++, as well as access to at least one web browser. See Chapter 1 for download information.

You will also need some various online reference guides, which I'll link to throughout the chapter.

## Optional Tools and Supplies

Although it's not required, you may want to have an additional book or handbook at your side, depending on your learning style. As mentioned previously, here are a few of my favorites:

*HTML and CSS* by Jon Duckett

*Build Your Own Website: A Comic Guide to HTML, CSS, and WordPress* by Nate Cooper with Art by Kim Gee

## Why Modify an Existing HTML Template?

As professional communicators, you won't often be called upon to create an HTML website from scratch. What you may be asked to do, however, is read existing HTML and CSS code, understand what it's saying, and edit/modify it for a new purpose or audience. To that end, knowing how to modify existing code is almost more valuable to technical communicators than coding everything by hand.

That's not to say that coding itself is not valuable; so far you've learned many beginning and intermediate coding skills in HTML5 and CSS3, and you can certainly learn more programming by pursuing more advanced coding topics.

However, in my experience, communicators don't have to

be excellent coders; we just need to know enough to get by. Leveraging existing free and open code to create your projects is one way you can showcase your intermediate to advanced skills in HTML5 and CSS3 without having to code a website all on your own. In some ways, using templates helps you follow the old adage: "Work smarter, not harder."

In addition, modifying an existing template is an excellent way to learn. You'll see more code than I could possibly introduce in this book, while getting exposed to many different coding styles and approaches.

Finally, modifying an existing template is an empowering experience, particularly for those new to HTML and CSS. You'll end up with a site that will "wow" you and your audience, without having to be an expert yourself. As far as I'm concerned, it's a win-win.

## Finding and Choosing a Template to Modify

By the end of this chapter, you will have built a custom HTML and CSS website. But first, you'll need to find and select a template to use.

## Step 1: Choose the Type of Website

Of course, you should first decide on what type of website you'd like to create. This will help direct the look, feel, style, and features you select in your template.

You may choose for yourself what type of website you create. However, I recommend that it's something that does *not* require any type of interactivity (such as commenting). This is because such features are advanced and require access to a server, a database, and expertise in additional coding languages such as JavaScript.

> *Note: If you'd like to create an interactive site and have the skills, time, and resources to build a server and database to do so, you're welcome to—but I won't have the time to cover that in this book. In the next chapter, I'll provide you with some additional ideas for moving forward.*

To that end, you have a few options for the type of website you'll create, which include but aren't limited to:

- A professional portfolio website.

- A personal website.

- A website for a product or service you'd like to offer.

You might also choose to build upon the same content you created for Chapter 6. It's entirely up to you, so long as your idea can be done with just using HTML and CSS.

## Step 2: Pick Your Template

This part may take you some time, as you'll want to sort through and find just the perfect site template for the content you'd like to put in it.

The closer the website is to what you ultimately would want the better—so keep a close eye on things like image placement, color themes, layout of the content, and so on.

**Resources for HTML5 and CSS Templates**

You're welcome to find an HTML template on your own online (search, for instance, for "Free HTML Templates"); however, here are some good places to start.

- **HTML5 Up**: A site offering free HTML5 website templates, using Creative Commons licensing. https://html5up.net/

- **Templated**: At the time of this publication, Templated offered nearly 900 free HTML5 templates to download, again using Creative Commons licensing. https://templated.co/

- Article: "**Free Responsive HTML5 CSS3 Website Templates**" by Bradley Nice. https://medium.com/level-up-web/free-responsive-html5-css3-website-templates-9c3938d62428

- Article: "**147 Free Simple Website Templates for Clean Sites Using HTML & CSS 2021**" by Colorlib. https://colorlib.com/wp/free-simple-website-templates/

- **OS Templates**: Free and paid website templates. https://www.os-templates.com/free-website-templates

The reason I like most of the above resources is that they offer free and open source templates that are often released under a Creative Commons license, meaning they've been built off the principles of open access knowledge and resources (see https://creativecommons.org/ for more information). This helps aid in creativity and innovation by sharing intellectual property with others.

They also have some pretty impressive looking website templates that you can use to make your own content shine.

Note that most of these will have a "Demo" option, so you can see an example of the website in use before you download the code.

## Step 3: Download the Template Files

Whichever template you choose, make sure you download *all* of the associated files—including HTML and CSS. Keep track of where you download them.

Then, using Windows Explorer or Finder, copy and paste all of those files into a new folder. You'll want to keep the original files separate, so that you can go back to them if you end up messing something up and breaking the code later on.

Name your new folder something you'll easily remember.

 *Note: Many websites will also have a page with instructions on using their templates. Be sure to save the link of where you download the files in case you need to come back to it later.*

❧

## Modifying the Template Files

The template you choose will ultimately determine exactly what you need to do with it to modify it as your own. However, for the purposes of your learning in this chapter, there are some things I suggest you consider.

Your ultimate goal is to demonstrate an advanced understanding of HTML and CSS coding. To that end, at a minimum in my opinion, you'll need to do the following:

- Modify, redesign, and write/edit content for a minimum of five **.html** files.

> *Note:* You may have chosen a template that is a responsive, one-page design, where — technically speaking — all of the code happens on the index.html page. That's okay. However, if that's the case, make sure you have at least five menu items that link to a minimum of five major portions of the page.

- Customize at least one **.css** stylesheet, with at least three major changes (e.g., font change, color change(s), alignment changes, and so on).

- Change the generic content (e.g., copyright notices, footers, headers, titles, logos, and so on) to suit your custom site/design.

- Also, use at least one intermediate HTML5/CSS3 element from Chapter 6 in your redesign, such as adding an image with alt text, a document, a video, a table, and/or a new menu.

- Be sure to save your files often.

*Tip: I recommend making copies of files if you're planning on making major changes —so you can go back to earlier versions, in case something gets messed up.*

With that said, don't be afraid to play with—and even break—the code. It will happen, and it will be a very valuable part of the learning process. Fiddle with the HTML tags, play around with the CSS, and then reload your page(s) to see what happens. This will be an exercise in trial and error, as well as in creativity and experimentation.

*Tip: The more often you test/refresh your testing page in a web browser, the easier it will be to locate any errors you make. I suggest doing so after each and every change you make, no matter how small.*

## A Few Additional Resources

As you work, you may need to reference some more intermediate HTML5 and CSS3 concepts than what was covered in the previous few chapters.

Here are a few resources that may be useful as you work through the code in your chosen template. I suggest that if you don't know a tag or element, look it up; if you don't understand something, search online, grab a book (I recommend a few in the introduction to this chapter), and/or use an Internet search to get some additional help.

MDN Web Docs: HTML (https://developer.mozilla.org/en-US/docs/Web/HTML): A resource that includes an overview of HTML from introductory to advanced concepts. It covers the HTML elements (tags), how to use them, and so on. They also have a handy HTML element reference page.

MDN Web Docs: CSS (https://developer.mozilla.org/en-US/docs/Web/CSS): Like the HTML reference, this site includes many tutorials and additional resources for learning and understanding CSS. You may particularly like their CSS reference page.

## Wow!

You can now consider yourself an expert in HTML5 and CSS3. (Okay, well, at least for the purposes of this book. At the very least, you can put it on your resume with confidence!)

To enhance your learning even further, now could be a good time to reflect on what you've learned, any issues or questions you've had so far, and what you'd like to learn moving forward. Try writing about your experiences in a journal, whether hard copy or something digital, such as in an app like Evernote or on a Trello board.

Be as specific as possible so you can come back and read this later, as documentation of how far you've come.

In the next chapter, we'll go over a few ideas of what to do next, including expanding your learning even further.

# CHAPTER 8
# BONUS RESOURCES
# AND ACTIVITIES

By now you should feel confident in knowing enough coding to get by in any communication context. You can confidently speak to coding on your resume and in job interviews. And you'll be able to communicate on the job with professional engineers and coders who will appreciate the understanding you bring to the rhetorical situation, as well as the advocacy you'll bring for the users of the products and software they're creating.

Pause for a moment and be proud of yourself for this accomplishment. Not everyone is willing to learn new things just to help further their professional relationships and communication abilities. Being open to consumer advocacy and interpersonal relationship building in a professional context is an amazing skill and one that will undoubtedly serve you well in any career you pursue. If you feel like you've learned enough to get by, then awesome; that was the goal! Hooray! You made it!

But let's just say for a minute you want to learn more. Perhaps you want to publish your own website or even just learn how to create more interactive HTML, CSS, and/or XML scripts for your personal or professional needs. This final chapter provides you with a few additional resources you can use to take your learning to the next level, including publishing your website, learning additional coding languages, and even exploring a new type of coding altogether.

## Publishing Your Website

People often ask me what tools I use to publish my websites. Whereas there are many other websites, articles, and books that cover this topic in more detail, here is what I use for my own websites.

> *Note: These recommendations are merely based off of my own experiences. I have not been paid or otherwise awarded for making these recommendations. Furthermore, I am not making any warranties implied or otherwise of their services, prices, etc. Use these ideas as a means of making your own decision about what's best for you.*

## Domain Name Registration

The first step in publishing your website is to choose and purchase a domain name.

I always suggest that people purchase their own name, such as carlyfinseth.com. If your name is already taken, you could try it with .org or another suffix instead of .com, or try your middle name, use a variant or fun spin, or even use a social media presence name or other nickname you've used in other circumstances.

Regardless of what you choose to name your website, you need to make sure it's available before you purchase it. This is called **domain name registration**.

My favorite domain name registration service is GoDaddy (https://www.godaddy.com/). Their prices are reasonable and they have good customer service if anything goes wrong with your website.

For other options, simply do an online search for "Domain Name Registration" and choose a company you think looks the best to you. You may also want to find a company that can not just sell you your domain name but also will provide website hosting if you need it. (That's the next step; see below.)

Any domain registration company you select should allow for free searches to find the right domain name that works for you.

## Web Hosting

The next thing you need is web hosting, or a place to host (store and backup) all of your HTML and CSS files, as well as images, documents, and so on that you use to build your site. This is usually found through a separate company that charges an annual or monthly fee for the storage space required (and traffic generated) to host your site.

Whereas GoDaddy does also provide web hosting—and an all-in-one service such as that is definitely an easy way to go— my favorite host for customer service is A Small Orange (https://asmallorange.com/). I have tried probably dozens of web hosts of the years and I have found A Small Orange to be the most reliable—meaning my website stays up nearly 100% of the time, which is *huge,* especially for an online business or professional website. They also have fast and responsive customer service and their hosting is relatively intuitive to figure out.

Regardless of what you choose, do an online search for "web hosting" and find one that best suits your needs. You want the company to have good pricing, solid customer support and reliability (so be sure to look up independent third-party reviews), and an intuitive interface for handling your files.

Another consideration is file space; new users should be able to use just about any starter plan, but if you have plans for large expansions or a huge amount of traffic to come to your site, you may think about buying a larger plan upfront. At the very least, look for a web host that will make it easy for you to upgrade or downgrade later, should your needs change.

Finally, think about whether it's important for you to have dedicated email addresses for your website (e.g., hello@yourwebsitehere.com or jane@yourwebsitehere.com). If so, you'll want to make sure your selected hosting plan includes email addresses and mail storage.

In short, there is no right or wrong solution as long as it feels right to you—but spend time on this part and find a service that resonates with you.

The reason why it's important to find a web host that works with your style is this is where you'll be uploading all of your created HTML5 and CSS3 files so you can publish them online. If the interface is difficult to figure out, it will make it that much more difficult for you to get started.

For example, some web hosts I've found almost dumb down the process too much. They want you to simply drag and drop an existing website they've already created into their hosting plan and do some basic modifications such as change the color or name. For me that doesn't work because I know how to code and want to modify my files myself. This is why I use an independent web host that allows me to upload my own code and images into their interface to create a custom website.

## File Transfer Protocol

Next, I recommend getting an **FTP**: short for File Transfer Protocol. FTP is simply a way of moving your files from your computer to your web host, so they'll show up on your website.

My favorite is Filezilla (https://filezilla-project.org/). It is a free server you download to your computer that allows you to connect to your web host and transfer your files through a simple interface.

Once you have a domain name, web hosting, and an FTP, you can login to your web hosting plan (and/or connect via FTP) and bring your files to life!

# Learning Interactive Coding

Now that you know the basics of XML, HTML5, and CSS, you may feel you want to learn more about interactive coding elements you can do to jazz up your websites and other deliverables.

Whether you're interested in learning how to provide a space for readers to provide comments on your blog posts, a safe space for users to communicate in an online forum, or adding interactive forms for users to provide feedback or even take quizzes or surveys, there are many ways you can dive into these topics to take your learning to the next level. Here are a few additional resources I recommend for the next step.

To get more advanced in your coding, the first thing I recommend is to learn some JavaScript. JavaScript is a common object-oriented computer programming langauge that will allow you to do more interactive things with your website. I've tried many resources and books on the subject and here are a few of my favorites:

*JavaScript and JQuery: Interactive Front-End Web Development* by **Jon Duckett**

> **Why you'd want it**: I'm a visual learner, so Jon Duckett's approach to programming is one that speaks to my nerdy little soul. If you enjoy reading a gorgeously-designed book while you're learning about complex programming concepts in easy-to-digest chunks, this is a good choice.

*JavaScript: The Definitive Guide: Master the World's Most-Used Programming Language* by **David Flanagan**

> **Why you'd want it**: If you're a completionist, this is a great option. This is a book published by O'Reilly, one of the most in-depth publishers for complex topics. If you don't want to learn just a little bit of JavaScript but want to learn *all the JavaScript*, including the hows, whys, and wheres... well, this book will be for you. This is probably the most comprehensive (and technical, sometimes *too* technical) titles I've found.

*Secrets of the JavaScript Ninja* by **John Resig, Bear Bibeault, and Josip Maras**

> **Why you'd want it**: If you learn best through storytelling and examples, this is the book for you. Secrets of the JavaScript Ninja will most appeal to readers who appreciate down-to-earth stories, scenarios, and examples to boost their learning about more technical concepts. This one also feels to me to be most like a college textbook in its voice and style—which could be good or bad, depending on your own personal preferences for learning.

All three of the above titles are available on Amazon.com and at other retailers.

## Bonus Activity: Learning Bootstrap

Up to this point, you've learned basic, intermediate, and advanced techniques in HTML5 and CSS3. Consider yourself ready to communicate about coding in just about any context!

In this section, I'll provide you with an additional optional activity to learn one more technology related to website publishing called **Bootstrap**.

## What is Bootstrap?

From the https://getbootstrap.com website:

> "Bootstrap is an open source toolkit for developing with HTML, CSS, and JS. Quickly prototype your ideas or build your entire app with our Sass variables and mixins, responsive grid system, extensive prebuilt components, and powerful plugins built on jQuery."

Okay, but explain it in English this time. What is Bootstrap?

Bootstrap is a collection of free and open source code that you can copy and paste into your own website designs. It includes HTML, CSS, and JavaScript (JS) and allows coders to quickly and easily use pre-built templates and plug-ins for design elements, such as fonts, forms, buttons, tables, image galleries, and more.

In other words, it's a collection of code you can legally "steal" to make your own work look awesome.

Bootstrap also helps web developers make responsive

websites, which are websites that respond in size based on the technologies that people are using to view it (e.g., smartphones, tablets, laptops, or desktops). Responsive websites are those that look good and function well on a screen of any size.

## Why Learn Bootstrap

Well, for starters because it's super cool. But also because (according to Bootstrap developers) it's "the most popular HTML, CSS, and JS library in the world" and (according to me) it's a hugely marketable skill/toolkit to add to your resume.

It also happens to be taught in every computer science program that I know of. Like other coding languages you explored in this book, Bootstrap is yet another skill that can help you better communicate with subject-matter experts (SMEs) in the workplace.

## How to Learn Bootstrap

Work through the below steps to get started with Bootstrap. See below on how to get and install Bootstrap.

Then, once you have Bootstrap downloaded to your computer, work through the scenario I provide below to test your understanding.

### Download and Unzip the Bootstrap Examples

Go to https://getbootstrap.com/docs/4.0/examples and click the button that says "Download source code." That will allow you to download a complete zip file of all .html and .css files for the examples shown on that page.

After it has downloaded, unzip the files so you can view/access them. If you don't know how to unzip a file, here's how:

- On a PC, open File Explorer and right-click on the zipped folder. Select "Extract All" and then follow the prompts.
- On a Mac, control-click on the zipped file you downloaded and then choose "Compress."

**Read the Scenario**

Here is the scenario you'll use when working with these files:

*You work for a small start-up and, although you were initially hired to write documentation, your job eventually grew to you handling some duties relating to user experience. You've done a few small usability studies and have determined the company's website needs a more responsive design, as well as some new features to make it more usable and appealing for your customers.*

- *Your boss has asked you to research and write up some specific ways that the website could be improved, and you came up with the following top priority items:*
- *You need to add a blog to better represetnt the friendly, hip vibe the company is going for, as well as share some fun tips and insider knowledge.*
- *The home page needs more visual interest, ideally in the form of a rotating carousel of images.*
- *The customers are having a hard time easily seeing the pricing structures and comparisons for your various products and services.*

- *The product page is clunky and confusing, and doesn't do a good job explaining what your company has to offer.*

*You've heard of Bootstrap and know you can use it to do any or all of the above features/improvements—and you've always wanted to learn. You decide to teach yourself Bootstrap to create a prototype of your idea for how to structure the website redesign. You want to include these prototypes in the report that you will send to your boss, so that they have a visual representation of your recommendations.*

## Pick a Bootstrap Example to Modify

After you've read the above scenario, decide which of the above priority item(s) you'd like to prototype as part of the scenario (e.g., blog, carousel, pricing structure, or product page). Pick at least one.

Browse the demos at https://getbootstrap.com/docs/4.0/examples; you may click through any of the images to see any of the examples in action. Once you find at least one you like, go back to the files you downloaded and find the corresponding .html and .css files by navigating to this folder on your computer:

```
Downloads > bootstrap-4.0.0 > docs >
4.0 > examples
```

For example, if you want to see the files for how to create the Carousel feature, you'd go to:

```
Downloads > bootstrap-4.0.0 > docs > 4.0 >
examples > carousel
```

Each example should have two files: an .html file and a corresponding .css file.

### Get Familiar with the Code

Next, open the **.html** file and the **.css** file in Notepad++ or another text editor of your choice.

Now, take a minute to read through the code and look at some of the conventions that make up Bootstrap.

First, note the standard Bootstrap code that is added within the header of the .html page. It looks like this:

```
<!-- Bootstrap core CSS -->
<link
href="../../../../dist/css/bootstrap.mi
n.css" rel="stylesheet">
```

This is the code that incorporates the core Bootstrap code into your .html page. Next, look at the custom styles comment that says:

```
<!-- Custom styles for this template -->
```

The code directly under that section is what is calling out (naming) the related .css stylesheet.

Finally, browse through the rest of the code, particularly where you see the word "class."

These are the places where the .html calls out the name of the .css designator so that it can style itself accordingly.

### Modify the Code and Create Your Prototype(s)

Now it's time to get your hands dirty. Use the Bootstrap .html and .css files to create a prototype solution for the scenario above.

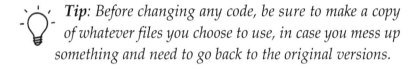

*Tip: Before changing any code, be sure to make a copy of whatever files you choose to use, in case you mess up something and need to go back to the original versions.*

Come up with a fictional company name and information. Write the fictional content, the menu items, headings and subheading, etc. That is, customize your example so that would look fancy-schmancy for the report you're giving to your boss.

Using the caveat above of making a copy of the original files, save your work as you go.

### Reflect on Your Learning

To complete the activity, write down what you learned from the exercise, including some of the possibilities (or limitations) you see with using Bootstrap. Do you think you'd use it in the future? Why or why not?

## Bonus Activity: Collaborative Coding and Version Control

As a technical communicator, one of my favorite parts about coding is the reminder that it's simply another form of writing. And, just like traditional writing, coding can be done individually or as part of a larger team.

To take your learning to the next level, consider how you might work on your coding as part of a team. Naturally, you would need a way to track who did what, what was changed, and even the ability to go back to other parts of your code if an error was introduced or if you wanted to go back to another version or feature of your code.

Such practices are called **version control** and are a standard practice for professional coders, whether they work as part of a team or not.

Version control allows you to collaboratively save, edit, and sync your work across platforms and with many people. It's most often used with coding/programming but is sometimes used in traditional writing contexts, as well. You're probably most familiar with Google Docs as one option for versioning, but in this bonus activity, you'll learn a more robust tool called Draft.

### What is Draft?

You may have heard of Git and GitHub. Git (https://git-scm.com/) is a versioning control system, which allows you to collaboratively track changes on your work without losing your data.

Git is most often used for coding, but can also be used for any other project that could benefit from saving multiple drafts without losing your work. GitHub (https://github.com/) is the platform most commonly used to host your Git versions.

Well, Draft is essentially GitHub that has been designed specifically for writers. It's a collaborative writing platform that lets you write, save, edit, version, and collaborate all in real time.

For this activity, you'll sign up for and explore Draft, which can help get you familiar with version control, whether you're writing a paper, a blog post, or HTML code.

## Sign Up for Draft

To participate in this activity, you'll first have to sign up for Draft. Go to www.draftin.com and follow the steps for signing up.

## Start a New Document

Once you have an account, click on "New Document." Then, take a look at the options on the left-hand menu. You can rename your document to whatever you like. Play a bit with the various buttons and find out how you can reorganize your writing.

## Learn Some Shortcuts

Once you start your first document, you'll notice a simple screen where you can write whatever comes to mind. Click on the dropdown in the upper-right corner to explore some shortcuts and hot keys you can use for formatting your text or code.

Spend some time writing some random things and then practicing some of the shortcuts. (If you need some dummy text to play with, see: www.lipsum.com.)

### Invite Others to Collaborate (Optional)

To really explore the power of version control, invite some friends to try it out with you. Do so using the top-left menu and clicking "Share."

### Decide What to Write... Then Start Writing!

If you already have an idea of what type of writing you would like to undertake, feel free to dive in. I suggest trying a creative writing piece, a blog post, a short report, a memo, or just about anything that can be written collaboratively. If you're not sure where to start, consider this fictional scenario:

> *Pretend that in the next year or so, you will be remodeling a large part of your house, but you will only have the time and money to remodel one room. Think about which room you'd remodel and why.*
>
> *Write up a short proposal that outlines your idea/choice of room, the benefits of choosing it (and perhaps any down sides), and your recommendations for what would need to be improved.*
>
> *Then, consider how you'd approach the remodel in terms of what you'd do first and why, and how you'd design the space.*

Once you have your idea, start writing! The idea of Draft is you can write and edit with others at the same time. Don't forget to save your work as you go; this will trigger a new version that you can go back and work on and/or approve later. *This is the heart of version control.*

You can see it in action on Draft by clicking on the numbered link in the upper-right that says "# DRAFTS."

Congratulations! You've now learned another key concept of coding, which is version control. Sure, you're not an expert in Git yet, but when the coders and engineers you work with start talking about it, you'll know understand the context but in a way that makes more sense for communicators. (Plus, it's a cool tool you can now use for your own writing.)

This also means that you know have the core foundation to go out and learn about Git and GitHub, should you so choose. If you're interested, here's a good place to start: https://guides.github.com/activities/hello-world/.

## The Key to All of This

We've come to the end of our learning journey in this book. (If you're a completionist, there's a Glossary after this but technically we're nearly done.) Thank you so much for choosing to spend your time with me. I'm humbled and honored to be your guide as you learn the basics of coding for communicators.

I am a strong advocate of lifelong learning. I truly believe the path to self-improvement lies in our own abilities and willingness to learn and grow—and to explore new opportunities and pathways that seem interesting and exciting to us.

If coding seems to be something that really gets you enthusiastic, creative, and inspired, then I am so happy you have found this! I encourage you to keep going and continue to challenge yourself toward new directions.

Of course, it's also just okay to stop here and be happy to let the engineers and coders do their thing, while you continue to communicate and advocate for a better world. No one will judge you for that, least of all me.

In short, congratulations on taking this next step to opening the door toward a career and lifetime filled with communication, collaboration, advocacy, and (hopefully) a bit of coding!

# GLOSSARY

## A

**<a>**: Used to signify a hyperlink in HTML. The <a> tag is most used with <href>, as in <a href>, as a way of pointing to files, email addresses, and websites. See also: <href>, Hyperlink.

**a:hover**: CSS3 that defines the properties of a link when a user hovers over it, such as color and pixel size.

**a:link**: CSS3 that defines the properties of a link without clicking on it or hovering over it.

**a:visited**: CSS3 that defines the properties of a link after a user has clicked on it.

**alt**: A descriptive element of the <img src> tag that describes for screen readers and other devices what the image is. Also useful for times when images may not load.

**<article>**: An HTML tag to indicate content that will be syndicated or reused elsewhere. End with </article>.

<aside>: An HTML tag to identify information that may digress from the rest of the content. End with </aside>.

# B

**<blockquote>**: HTML code to inset text with a tabbed look. Use </blockquote> to end the inset text.

**<body>**: Indicates in an HTML document where the header information ends and the body of text begins. Use </body> to end the section.

**Bootstrap**: A collection of free and open source code that you can copy and paste into your own website designs.

**border-collapse**: CSS that allows you to define whether you want the borders in your table to be separated or shared. Border-collapse: separate will separate them, while border-collapse: collapse will make them shared.

**<br />**: HTML code that creates a line break.

# C

**cellpadding**: A callout for an HTML table that creates additional spacing between the walls of cells and the content inside.

**cellspacing**: A callout for an HTML table that creates additional spacing between table cells.

**Comment Tags**: Used in HTML and CSS to leave notes for yourself. In HTML they look like this: <!-- Content here --> In CSS they look like this: /* Content here */

**Conditional Tags**: A concept that allows you to show some parts of your XML content in some outputs but not others.

**Cross-Reference**: A way of linking from one XML document to another.

**CSS (Cascading Style Sheet)**: Code that is used to add visual design to your webpages.

**CSS3 (Cascading Style Sheet, 3rd Revision)**: The latest version of CSS.

# D

**Debugging**: Discovering and correcting errors in your code.

**Declaration Block**: CSS3 code that goes between these two curly brackets: { } .

**Declarations**: The part of CSS3 that declares what we want our HTML5 code to look like.

**<div>**: An outdated method of defining structure and layout on an HTML page. Today it's better to use other tags, such as <header>, <main>, and <section>.

**Domain Name Registration**: Naming, purchasing, and registering an URL for your website.

**Draft**: The name of a software versioning tool for writers. See also: Git, GitHub, and version control.

## E

****: An HTML5 tag used to italicize text. Use  to end the italics.

**em**: The commonly accepted standard for calling out font size in CSS3. Example: 2em is two times the normal viewing size on a particular screen.

**End Tag**: A type of tag that ends a section of code. It looks like this: </tag>.

## F

**<footer>**: Used in HTML to designate the bottom footer portion of a website. End with </footer>.

**Formatting**: A way of using XML to give your data style and design, such as font style, background color, or bolding/italics.

**FTP (File Transfer Protocol)**: A way of moving your files from your computer to your web host so they'll show up on your website.

## G

**Git**: A versioning control system common with professional coders. See also: version control.

**GitHub**: The platform most commonly used to host Git versions.

# H

**<h1>**: HTML code for calling out a level 1 heading. End the heading with </h1>. You may also use <h2>, <h3>, and so on.

**<head>**: Indicates the header portion of an entire HTML document. Use </head> to end the section.

**<header>**: The place for a title and heading information for the content within an HTML page. End with </header>.

**Hex Code (Hexadecimal Color Code)**: A portion of code that starts with a # followed by six letters and numbers that refer to a specific color combination of RGB (red, green, and blue). Example: #D9BEE7.

**<hr />**: HTML code that creates a horizontal rule.

**<href> (Hypertext Reference)**: Used in HTML code to specify links and paths to additional content. See also: <a>, Hyperlink.
 <html>: A tag to start your HTML document. Use </html> to end your document.

**HTML (Hypertext Markup Language)**: A coding language used to format and write content for the Internet. See also: HTML5.

**HTML5 (Hypertext Markup Language, 5th Revision)**: An extensible, customizable version of HTML, currently in its fifth revision. See also: HTML.

**HTTP (Hypertext Transfer Protocol)**: The letters at the beginning of a URL that allow the computer to retrieve or transfer content from across the Internet. See also: HTTPS.

**HTTPS (Secure Hypertext Transfer Protocol)**: A secure version of HTTP, often used on websites that use and/or store secure information, such as payment information or passwords. See also: HTTP.

**Hyperlink**: A link to an email address or website. See also <a> and <href>.

# I

**<img src>**: An HTML tag that declares you want to insert an image, and then tell the computer where to get it (source it). index.html: Your primary HTML page.

# J-K

**JavaScript**: An object-oriented programming language that allows for more advanced and interactive elements for a website, including commenting, discussions, surveys, and quizzes.

# L

**<li>**: HTML code for a list item for either a bulleted or numbered list. End each list item with </li>. See also: <ol> and <ul>.

**<link>**: An HTML tag that tells the computer to link one document or stylesheet to another.

# M

**<main>**: The tag for placing all of your primary HTML website content. End with </main>.

**main.css**: Your primary CSS document.

**Markup Language**: A coding language used primarily for the web, consisting of rules and tags as a way of categorizing, processing, and presenting information. Examples include XML, XHTML, and HTML.

# N

**<nav>**: Short for navigation, this HTML tag is used to create hierarchical navigation, such as a menu or a Table of Contents. End with </nav>.

**nth-child**: In CSS, the exact number of columns from left to right that you want to format.

# O

**<ol>**: HTML code for starting a numbered list. Use </ol> to end the list. Also see: <li>.

# P-Q

**<p>**: Starts a new paragraph in HTML. Use </p> to end your paragraph.

**padding**: In CSS, the amount of space, in pixels, you want all around your content.

**Properties**: The first part of a CSS3 declaration. Includes things such as background-color, font-family, and font-size.

# R

**rel="stylesheet"**: "Rel" stands for relationship; this code specifies the relationship between an HTML document and its accompanying CSS.

# S

**<section>**: The HTML tag that defines a chunk of content or information that belongs together. End with </section>. Can also be used with <h1>, <h2>, etc.

**Selectors**: What CSS3 uses to select a certain amount of content in the HTML5 code. It's the part that comes before the opening curly cue brackets that look like this: { .

**Single-Sourcing**: A way to manage and organize content so that a single source of information can be used to publish artifacts in multiple ways (e.g., print and digital formats).

**Start Tag**: A type of tag that starts a section of code. It looks like this: <tag>.

****: An HTML code to signify bold text. Use  to end the bold text.

**Stylesheet Declaration**: A line of code in your XML document that tells your computer where and how to find your XSL stylesheet.

# T

**<table>**: Creates a table in HTML. Use </table> to end your table.

**table-layout:** CSS that specifies the widths of the columns in your table. Options include table-layout: fixed or table-layout: auto.

**Tag**: A portion of code enclosed within two brackets, like this < >.

**target="_blank"**: A hyperlink callout that tells the computer to open the link in a new tab. See also: <a>, <href>, and Hyperlink.

**Targets**: A concept used for defining an output for your XML project, such as PDF or Word document.

**<tbody>**: Creates body content in an HTML table. Use </tbody> to end the table body content.

**<td>**: Creates a new cell in a row of an HTML table. Use </td> to end the cell.

**text-align**: CSS that calls out your preferred alignment for the text, either: left, right, or center.

**Text Editor**: Technology or software used to edit text. Commonly used for writing and editing code.

**Text Inset**: A way of inserting XML content from an external source into Adobe Framemaker.

**<th>**: Creates a new header in an HTML table. Use </th> to end the header.

**<thead>**: Groups the header in an HTML table with the rest of the table contents. End with </thead>. See also: <th>.

**<title>**: The tag used to set the title of your webpage. Use </title> to end the title.

**<tr>**: Creates a new row in an HTML table. Use </tr> to end the row.

**Transforming**: A way of using XML to translate data into your preferred format (e.g., PDF or HTML).

## U

**<ul>**: HTML code for starting a bulleted list. Use </ul> to end the list. Also see: <li>.

**URI/URL (Uniform Resource Identifier/Uniform Resource Locator)**: Commonly referred to as URLs, these are addresses you type into your web browser to visit a specific website.

# V

**Values**: Specific CSS3 styles we want to apply. Examples include hex codes, individual fonts, and font sizes.

**Variable**: A name you use in coding to refer to a specific value. Sometimes referred to as name-value.

**Version Control**: The ability to track changes in your code, as well as go back to (revert) to previous versions as and if necessary.

# W

**Web Hosting**: A place to host (store and backup) all of your website code, images, and files.

**Web Safe Font**: A font that is universally considered to be loadable on everyone's computer and therefore usable on the web.

**WWW (World Wide Web)**: An old school way of referring to the Internet. Sometimes still used as a way of inputting a website; e.g., www.google.com.

# X-Z

**XHTML (eXtensible Hypertext Markup Language)**: A now mostly retired coding language originally designed to make HTML more customizable but since replaced with HTML5.

**XML (eXtensible Markup Language)**: A coding language used to communicate and organize data that can be extended to suit your customized needs. It is most commonly used for single-sourcing technical communication content in digital and print format.

**XML Declaration**: The first line of XML code in your XML document. It is required, as it tells your computerwhat version of XML you're using and what to do with the code.

**XML Document**: The file you use to write, organize, and name your data. Ends with .xml.

**XML Editor**: Software that allows the user to easily write and edit XML code.

**XMLNS (XML Namespace)**: A line of code in your XML document that declares which naming conventions you've used in your document.

**XSL Stylesheet**: The file you use to transform and format your XML data. Ends with .xsl.

# ABOUT THE AUTHOR

## Dr. Carly Finseth

Carly Finseth, Ph.D. is a multiple award-winning educator, author, researcher, and consultant.

Her academic expertise is in technology, writing, and games-based learning. Her industry background includes executive leadership, project management, and editing and publications management. She was a freelance writer, editor, web developer, and designer for nearly 20 years. Since 2017 she has been the Founder & CEO of Finseth Educational Consulting LLC.

She lives with her husband and son in beautiful Boise, Idaho.

# ADDITIONAL BOOKS
# BY THIS AUTHOR

## Teach Like a Gamer: Adapting the Instructional Design of Digital Role-Playing Games

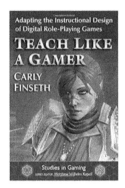

Digital role-playing games such as *Rift*, *Diablo III*, and *Kingdoms of Amalur: Reckoning* help players develop skills in critical thinking, problem solving, digital literacy, and lifelong learning. The author examines both the benefits and the drawbacks of role-playing games and their application to real-world teaching techniques. Readers will learn how to incorporate games-based instruction into their own classes and workplace training, as well as approaches to redesigning curriculum and programs.